Relative Justice

Relative Justice

CULTURAL DIVERSITY, FREE WILL,
AND MORAL RESPONSIBILITY

Tamler Sommers

PRINCETON UNIVERSITY PRESS
PRINCETON AND OXFORD

Copyright © 2012 by Princeton University Press

Published by Princeton University Press,
41 William Street, Princeton, New Jersey 08540
In the United Kingdom: Princeton University Press,
6 Oxford Street, Woodstock, Oxfordshire OX20 1TW

press.princeton.edu

Library of Congress Cataloging-in-Publication Data
Sommers, Tamler, 1970–
  Relative justice : cultural diversity, free will, and moral responsibility /
Tamler Sommers.
      p. cm.
  Includes bibliographical references (p.) and index.
  ISBN 978-0-691-13993-7 (hardcover : alk. paper)
  1. Responsibility—Cross-cultural studies.   2. Skepticism.
  3. Ethics.   I. Title.
  BJ1451.S67 2012
  170'.42—dc22   2011014067

British Library Cataloging-in-Publication Data is available

This book has been composed in Minion Pro

Printed on acid-free paper. ∞

Printed in the United States of America
10   9   8   7   6   5   4   3   2   1

For my father, Fred Sommers,

---

and for the memory of my mother, Shula Sommers

The statement, therefore, that men can be held responsible solely for individual conduct freely willed is certainly wrong; it mistakes a principal characteristic of individualistic ages for an eternal law of human nature.

—*Heinrich Gomperz, "Individual, Collective, and Social Responsibility"*

CONTENTS

ACKNOWLEDGMENTS

The first time I presented a paper on this book's thesis was at the "Conference on Responsibility, Agency, and Persons at the University of San Francisco," organized by Manuel Vargas. I was one of six lucky junior philosophers to present, and each of us received extensive comments from an accomplished scholar or "free will celebrity" (as Manuel called them). John Martin Fischer, a free will celebrity by any standard, was my commentator and his criticisms helped to shape the project as it developed. Thanks to John and so many of the other senior philosophers in our field for creating such a congenial and supportive environment. Thanks also to Manuel for indulging me in several long conversations about issues in metaethics and the philosophy of language. Several key sections of the book have benefited tremendously from these discussions.

Shaun Nichols has offered important suggestions and much encouragement throughout the writing process. His own work has been a source of inspiration for many of the arguments and my general approach in this project. I am deeply grateful for his generosity, friendship, and support.

I owe a huge debt of thanks to Saul Smilansky for his extensive, in-depth comments on earlier drafts of this book. My arguments have been significantly refined and (I hope) improved as a result of his criticisms. Thanks also to Ron Mallon for valuable comments on an earlier draft—and for helping me to curb my excessive use of abbreviations. And thanks to Derk Pereboom for his important contributions during the early stages of this project, and for introducing me to the complex view of responsibility in the Old Testament.

Thanks to John Doris, Joshua Knobe, Michael McKenna, Eddy Nahmias, Stephen Stich, and Jonathan Weinberg for many helpful comments and suggestions about this project. I am also grateful to Steve Burks, and Mark Collier—my colleagues at the University of Minnesota, Morris—and to Bill Nelson, Dave Phillips, and Josh Weisberg at the University of Houston for valuable discussions on the book's topic.

Many of the ideas in this book were floated on the free will blog "The Garden of Forking Paths" and its later incarnation "Flickers of Freedom." The discussions that followed were enormously helpful and I am grateful for all of them. There are too many contributors on those blogs to name, but I would like to offer special thanks to Tom Clark and Thomas Nadelhoffer for their comments on my post "[To Hell With] the TNR Principle," which I address in the final chapter of this book.

I am grateful to Rob Tempio, philosophy editor at Princeton University Press for his encouragement and advice at every stage of this process, and for finding such excellent reviewers. And much thanks to Eva Jaunzems for her fantastic work in the copyediting of this book.

Several passages and arguments have been adapted from my earlier work. Thanks to *Philosophy Compass, Philosophy and Phenomenological Research, Biology and Philosophy,* and the *Philosophical Quarterly* for allowing me to use that material here.

As always, I wish to express my love and gratitude to my wife Jennifer and my daughter Eliza for their support and encouragement, for making our house a pleasant place to work and, more importantly, a wonderful place to stop working. Finally, it breaks my heart to note that this will be the last project that was conceived, planned, shaped, and revised during long walks with Tess, the best dog anyone could ask for.

Houston, Texas
March 2011

Relative Justice

INTRODUCTION

METASKEPTICISM ABOUT MORAL RESPONSIBILITY

Just after the shootings at Virginia Tech University, a reporter for the National Public Radio program *Day to Day* set out to interview Koreans living in Los Angeles about the massacre. At first the reporter had trouble finding anyone who was willing to answer her questions. Some actually fled from the microphone. Finally, a Korean realtor agreed to be interviewed. He claimed to be deeply ashamed about the incident. The reporter was incredulous: "Why?" she asked him. "You had nothing to do with it!" The man replied, "I know, but he was a fellow Korean."[1]

In the same week Rev. Dong Sun Lim, founder of the Oriental Mission Church in Koreatown, released this statement: "All Koreans in South Korea—as well as here—must bow their heads and apologize to the people of America." And South Korean Ambassador Lee Taesik called on Korean Americans not just to be ashamed, but to repent. He suggested a thirty-two-day fast, one day for each victim of the carnage.

Many Americans found this attitude baffling. Why should Koreans living thousands of miles away from Blacksburg, Virginia, feel compelled to apologize, never mind starve themselves, for something over which they had no control? What did they have to apologize *for*? Adrian Hong, a board member of the Mirae

Foundation, a national organization of Korean-American college students, offers this explanation:

> First-generation Koreans tend to have a cultural sense of shared responsibility. If something good happens to one, it happens to all Koreans, and if something bad happens to one, it happens to all of them. [2]

UCLA anthropology professor Kyeyoung Park adds:

> In Western culture there is an emphasis on guilt; in many Eastern cultures the emphasis is on shame. I think Korean-Americans want to do something [about the incident] because they feel ashamed. Some of them feel *truly responsible*, even though it is ridiculous to think they are responsible for the action of this person.[3] (italics added)

The Koreans' sense of shared blame, along with the failure of many Americans to understand it, is one example of variation in perspectives about moral responsibility across cultures. Many of these differences concern beliefs about the *conditions* or *criteria* for fair assignment of blame and praise. The incredulity of the *Day to Day* reporter—"But you had nothing to do with it!"—illustrates the common Western intuition that moral responsibility has a robust control condition: in order to be genuinely blameworthy for a state of affairs, you must have played an active role in bringing it about. This intuition is so deeply embedded in the Western individualistic belief system that it seems self-evident, like a mathematical truth or an elementary rule of logic. But like other intuitions and beliefs about moral responsibility, it is not nearly as universal as we might think.

These cultural differences are not merely interesting from an anthropological perspective. They are also philosophically significant—deeply relevant, I will argue, to contemporary debates about moral responsibility. This is because (1) contemporary philosophical theories of moral responsibility develop *universal* conditions for fair assignments of blame and praise; and (2) they appeal to intuitions about cases and principles to justify these conditions. Consequently, these theories rely (at least implicitly) on empirical assumptions about the universality of the intuitions to which they appeal. In this book, I will develop an empirical and philosophical challenge to this assumption, one that if successful casts doubt on the prospect of establishing any theory of responsibility as objectively correct.

PLAN OF THE BOOK

Chapter 1 examines the methodology that philosophers employ to defend their theories of moral responsibility, and reveals the ways in which they rely on appeals to intuition. I also show that most leading theories aspire to universality; that is, they aim to provide conditions for moral responsibility that hold for human beings across cultures. I then identify the crucial empirical assumptions upon which theories of moral responsibility rely because of these common features.

The next three chapters develop my challenge to these assumptions by examining evidence for cross-cultural variation in intuitions about the conditions for moral responsibility. Chapter 2 focuses on the norms, attitudes, and practices of groups commonly referred to as "honor cultures." Chapter 3 examines literature highlighting the differences between "individualist" societies (e.g., the United States, Great Britain, and Western Europe) and "collectivist societies" (e.g., Japan, China, and South Korea). I survey literature from a wide variety of disciplines, including anthropology, social psychology, cultural psychology, sociology, and classical literature. My overarching goal is to give the reader a taste of how differently human beings have regarded moral responsibility across cultures and throughout history.

Of course, some defenders of objectivity or universality are happy to concede the existence of this variation. But they claim that the differences can be explained away as the products of irrationality, superstition, conceptual ambiguity, or ignorance about non-moral facts. According to this view, some cultures are simply mistaken about the conditions for moral responsibility, just as some cultures are mistaken about geological or biological facts. In the search for the truth about responsibility, what matters are the attitudes of "fully informed" individuals operating under more ideal conditions of rationality. Such fully informed individuals would share common judgments and attitudes regarding the conditions of moral responsibility, and it is *those* judgments that either constitute the truth or guide us to the truth about moral responsibility.

I believe this is the most promising strategy available for defending universalist or objectivist theories of moral responsibility. Its success, however, is dependent on a crucial empirical assumption. Specifically, the assumption that under ideal conditions of rationality human beings would come to share considered intuitions about moral responsibility *whatever their physical and social environment.* In chapter 4, perhaps the most important chapter in the book, I raise serious doubts about the plausibility of this assumption by examining the origins of these intuitive differences and the psychological mechanisms that underlie them. I review recent theories in the evolution of cooperation, which suggest that a wide variety of norms may emerge as a response to the different features of a culture's social and physical environment. I then appeal to theories about the psychology of norm acquisition to argue that variation in norms about responsibility is grounded in cognitive mechanisms associated with emotional responses and intuitions about deserv-ingness. Since our attitudes and norms are grounded in the deep-est levels of our cognitive psychologies, which in turn are shaped by our social and physical environment, I conclude that it is unlikely that we would ever reach agreement about the criteria of moral responsibility—even under ideal conditions of ratio-nality. Since there will always be variation in human environ-ments, there will be always be significant variation in the core starting intuitions that form the basis of our considered, reflec-tive judgments about moral responsibility.

By the end of chapter 4, I will have presented evidence that there are significant differences in intuitions about moral respon-sibility across cultures, and that at least some of these differences are not resolvable by rational argument or philosophical analysis. Since theories of moral responsibility ultimately stand or fall ac-cording to their intuitive plausibility, I conclude that there is no set of conditions for moral responsibility that applies universally, and therefore that no theory of moral responsibility is objectively correct. This challenge applies not only to positive accounts of moral responsibility, but also to skeptical or nihilistic theories, which claim that human beings *everywhere* cannot deserve praise or blame. Consequently, I have labeled my position *metaskepti-cism about moral responsibility.*[4]

Part Two of the book examines the implications of metaskep-ticism. Chapter 5 compares metaskepticism and other non-tra-ditional views of moral responsibility, focusing especially on the work of Richard Double. I then sketch out a methodology for arriving at settled beliefs about moral responsibility, given the truth of metaskepticism. I argue that although no theory can be objectively or universally true, there are principled ways in which we can approach moral responsibility within our own social, cul-tural, and psychological frameworks. The chapter concludes with a discussion of four factors that must be taken into account if we are to arrive at reasonable relativized judgments about the conditions for blame and praise.

My final two chapters apply these factors in an attempt to reach the most reasonable all-things-considered judgment for people in individualistic societies who share my starting intuitions. These chapters are in large part programmatic. Their primary goal is to illustrate how one can evaluate different positions on moral responsibility while remaining consistent with the metaskeptical thesis. Chapter 6 considers arguments in favor of restricted versions of libertarianism and compatibilism. Chapter 7 examines the case for first-order skepticism or eliminativism about moral responsibility, and offers a very tentative endorsement of this position in the context of our environment, historical period, and circumstances.

PART I

Metaskepticism about
Moral Responsibility

CHAPTER ONE

The Appeal to Intuition

Why Variation Matters

When describing the thesis of this book, I occasionally hear a version of the following complaint:

> "Who cares about people's intuitions about free will and moral responsibility? I'm interested in the *truth* about free will and moral responsibility. Your project doesn't tell me anything about that!"

This kind of objection has a sensible ring. In debates over, say, group selection in evolutionary theory, we do not examine folk intuitions about how Darwinian natural selection might work. We consider these intuitions to be largely irrelevant in our theorizing. Why shouldn't level-headed philosophers regard free will and moral responsibility the same way?

The answer is simple: unlike evolutionary biologists, philosophers have thus far investigated the nature of their topic through an appeal to the intuitions of their audience. The goal of this chapter is to illustrate the ways in which philosophical theories of moral responsibility depend on appeals to intuitions for justification, and then to show how these theories must make certain empirical assumptions about the nature of these intuitions.

WHAT DO I MEAN BY "MORAL RESPONSIBILITY"?

Some definitions are in order. 'Moral responsibility' means different things to different people. The sense of moral responsibility that I am concerned with here is the "desert-entailing" variety (Strawson 1986). To believe that someone is morally responsible for an action in this sense is to believe that the person *deserves* blame or praise and perhaps punishment or reward. The meaning of "desert" is another tricky issue with no precise resolution. I interpret it in the non-consequentialist sense that is common in the literature: Agent A deserves blame (or praise or punishment or a reward)" if and only if A ought to be blamed (praised/punished/rewarded) independent of any practical or consequentialist benefits that may arise from doing so. Another way to describe this feature of desert is that someone deserves blame or punishment when it is *fair* or *appropriate* to blame or punish them (Wallace 1994). Although the term "moral responsibility" is used in many other ways, it is this desert-entailing sense that is at the center of the philosophical debate. No one denies that consequentialist benefits can arise from holding people morally responsible, and therefore that consequentialist interpretations of moral responsibility are compatible with determinism. The philosophical disagreement has focused on whether non-consequentialist, desert-entailing responsibility is justifiable in light of a deterministic or naturalistic understanding of human behavior.

What Do I Mean by "Intuition"?

Following Nichols, et al. (2003), I use the term "intuition" to refer to "a spontaneous judgment about the truth or falsity of a proposition—a judgment for which the person making the judgment *may* be able to offer little or no further justification (my italics)."[1] I stress "may" because people can hold some intuitions that are supported by other considerations. When I refer to intuitions that have been held up to critical scrutiny, I will use the term "considered intuitions"—in contrast to "starting intuitions," which refer to initial judgments or responses that get the process of reflective equilibrium rolling. Philosophical theories of moral responsibility rely on appeals to both types of intuitions, although most aim to capture considered intuitions, formed upon reflection with knowledge of the relevant facts.

"Universalist" Theories of Moral Responsibility

The large majority of theories about moral responsibility aim to provide conditions or criteria for moral responsibility that apply universally, for all agents, for all societies. By this I do not mean that the theories conclude that all (or even any) adults in a given society can be morally responsible for their behavior. It may be that no member of a particular culture can meet the theory's criteria for justified assignments of blame and praise. It may even be that no member of *any* culture can meet the criteria, as skeptics like Galen Strawson (1986) and Derk Pereboom (2001) believe. But the conditions or criteria *themselves* are meant to apply across cultures in such a way that if the sufficient conditions specified in the theory are met, the agent is morally responsible for the behavior; and if the necessary conditions are not met, the agent is not responsible. I refer to theories that posit universal criteria for moral responsibility as "universalist" theories and my challenge is directed primarily to them. My claim is that if the theories are meant to apply across cultures, and they ultimately rely on appeals to intuition for justification, the theories must make implicit assumptions about the universality of the intuitions to which they appeal.

INCOMPATIBILIST APPEALS TO INTUITION

Incompatibilists about moral responsibility hold that if causal determinism is true, no one can deserve blame or praise for his or her character or behavior. They divide into two very different groups. *Libertarians* claim that we can be responsible for our behavior and so determinism must be false. *Skeptics* (also referred to as nihilists, eliminativists, or hard incompatibilists) deny that we can be morally responsible for our behavior, either because they are determinists, or, more commonly, because they hold that any plausible understanding of human behavior (deterministic or indeterministic) is incompatible with moral desert.

Arguments for incompatibilism generally employ at least one of two key principles to show that the conditions for moral responsibility cannot be satisfied if determinism is true.

1. The *Principle of Alternate Possibilities* (PAP): We cannot be morally responsible for an act if we lack the ability to do otherwise.

2. The *Transfer of Non-Responsibility* (TNR) *Principle*: We cannot be morally responsible for an act if we are not morally responsible for any of the determining factors of that act. (The non-responsibility for the determining factors "transfers" to the act itself.)[2]

In support of these principles, incompatibilists often appeal directly to their own intuitions and the intuitions of the reader. Van Inwagen, for example, offers the following defense of the TNR principle, which he refers to as "Rule B":[3]

> I must confess that my belief in the validity of [The TNR principle] has only two sources, one incommunicable and the other inconclusive. The former source is what philosophers are pleased to call "intuition." . . . The latter source is the fact that I can think of no instances of [the TNR Principle] that have, or could possibly have, true premises and a false conclusion. (Van Inwagen 1983, 97–99)

In fact, Van Inwagen's two sources are really quite similar, since someone with radically different intuitions from Van Inwagen's could come up with counterexamples rather easily. Anyone with the intuition that an agent in a particular case is morally responsible for a state of affairs he *clearly* could not have prevented would simply use that case as a counterexample to Van Inwagen's TNR principle. Consider a man, for example, who intuitively deemed himself blameworthy for his great-grandfather's treatment of slaves. This assignment of moral responsibility would be a counterexample to Rule B.[4]

Van Inwagen then issues a challenge to his compatibilist critics, one that serves as a nice illustration of the crucial role that intuitions play in their debate:

> If the compatibilist wishes to refute the direct argument here is what he will have to do. . . . He will have to produce some set of propositions intuitively more plausible than [the TNR principle] and show that these propositions entail the compatibility of moral responsibility and determinism, or he will have to offer a counterexample to

> [the TNR principle], a counterexample that can be evaluated independently of the question of whether moral responsibility and determinism are compatible. (Van Inwagen 1983, 188)

Compatibilists have generally selected the second strategy, attempting to develop intuitively plausible counterexamples to both TNR and PAP. The most famous of these is Frankfurt's (1969) case of Jones the assassin, featuring (of course) an evil neuroscientist by the name of Black. Black has placed a chip in Jones's brain, ensuring that he will murder a prime minister even if he has some last minute scruples that would otherwise cause him to abandon the plan. Because of the chip, Jones cannot do other than assassinate the prime minister. The assassination is determined to occur one way or the other. Frankfurt then argues that accepting PAP entails a counterintuitive conclusion—namely, that even if Black does nothing and Jones carries out his intention of killing the prime minister, Jones is not morally responsible for that act (because he lacked the ability to do otherwise). My aim is certainly not to take sides on the question of whether or not this is an effective counterexample. Rather it is to emphasize that *if* it is an effective counterexample, it must be so in virtue of how well it accords with the reader's intuitions about Jones's blameworthiness. Frankfurt-style examples do not reveal a logical inconsistency in the incompatibilist position. It is *logically* open for the incompatibilist to respond: "Well, Jones could not have done otherwise; therefore PAP is violated and he is not morally responsible—I stand by that." This conclusion would not be false exactly. Rather, it would (arguably) be *disingenuous* because even incompatibilists cannot find it intuitive that the mere placing of the chip in Jones' brain excuses Jones for his behavior even when the chip plays no role in causing it.[5]

The success of Frankfurt cases in undermining PAP has shifted the focus of the debate to the more powerful TNR principle. Attempting to undermine TNR, Fischer and Ravizza (1998) have developed cases in which a bad event is overdetermined in such a way that the agent's malicious actions and intentions do not end up causing the bad event. In the "erosion case," a woman named Betty tries to destroy a village by setting explosives to cause an avalanche. Her actions turn out not to cause the avalanche because at the same moment, the erosion of a glacier causes the avalanche to occur anyway. As it happens, then, Betty is not even partly responsible for any of the factors that led to the destruction of the village. Yet according to Fischer and Ravizza, we still blame Betty for the destruction of the village, because she was trying to bring about the bad event and her behavior (setting explosives to cause an avalanche) *would* have caused the destruction of the village had it not been for the glacier. There are a number of objections one could raise about this example, but note that it cannot hope to undermine the TNR principle unless the reader finds it intuitively plausible that Betty is morally responsible for the destruction of the village in the overdetermination cases.

Generalization Strategies

Van Inwagen's appeals to intuition are direct: he presents a principle that he finds intuitively obvious and challenges compatibilists to either come up with a more intuitively plausible principle or develop counterexamples. Strawson's (1986, 1994) "basic argument" is another example of such an appeal. Pereboom (1995, 2001) develops a more indirect strategy to defend the TNR principle, one that employs what Wallace (1994) calls "a generalization strategy." Pereboom describes three cases designed to become progressively more like ordinary determined human behavior. In each case, common compatibilist conditions are met, but we do not (according to Pereboom) deem the agent to be morally responsible. Pereboom's contention is that the "incompatibilist intuition"—the view that we are not responsible for acts that can be traced back to factors beyond our control (i.e., the TNR principle)—is the best explanation for our judgments in these cases. He then argues that there is no relevant difference between the third case and the fourth case, a human being living in a world where determinism or some form of naturalism about human behavior is true. He challenges the compatibilist to locate in his series of cases the relevant feature that would make the agent responsible for his or her behavior. According to Pereboom, the incompatibilist intuition best explains our judgments in the first three cases, and so we should apply it to the fourth as well.

It should be clear that appeals to intuition play a central role in this strategy. It cannot get off the ground unless the reader shares Pereboom's intuition about the non-responsibility of the agents in each of the first three cases. In order to undermine the argument, one must meet Pereboom's challenge: one must explain what the relevant difference is between the fourth case, ordinary human behavior, and the third. (Or, if the agent in the third case is deemed responsible, one must identify the relevant difference between that case and the second case.) And in order to evaluate whether the differences are relevant to appropriate assignments of moral responsibility, it is necessary to consult one's own intuitions. Mele (2005), for example, argues that the intuition that the agents are not responsible in the first three cases can be explained by the fact that there is a conscious manipulator in those cases. Pereboom (2005) responds by imagining a case where the manipulator is replaced by machines that randomly form in space, and claims that we still (intuitively) judge that the agents in those cases are not responsible. Again, my goal here is not to resolve this dispute but simply to point out that every move within it features an explicit appeal to our intuitions.

COMPATIBILIST APPEALS TO INTUITION

Compatibilists are no less reliant on appeals to intuitions, both to develop counterexamples to incompatibilist principles and to develop and refine compatibilist conditions for morally responsible behavior. The structure of Wolf's (1987) argument for her "sane deep self view" is a representative example of the role of intuitions in compatibilist theorizing. Wolf, like most of her contemporaries, is dissatisfied with the conditions of freedom and responsibility proposed by the so-called "classical compatibilists"—which boil down to the absence of constraints and the ability to act according to our desires. She finds the more sophisticated compatibilism of Frankfurt and Watson to be an improvement, but not quite sufficient. Frankfurt (1971) proposes that in order to have free will, we must be able to desire what we desire. To perform an act of our own free will, and be responsible for that act, we have to (1) be able to act according to our desire, and (2) have a second order desire that endorses the first order effective desire. Thus, an unwilling addict—someone who doesn't *want* to have the desire to do cocaine every time it is available—would lack free will because he does not have the will he wants to have. By contrast, people who endorse their first-order desire for cocaine—whether or not they are addicted—do the drug of their own free will and are morally responsible for doing so. For they are able to act according to the will they want to have.[6] Watson (1975) offers a variation of Frankfurt's view, arguing that free and responsible actions result from desires that are, in addition, *values*—desires, in other words, that we find to be good or worthwhile.

Wolf calls the views of Frankfurt's and Watson's "deep self views" and agrees that the views mark an important advance over classical compatibilist theories. But she argues that they fail to lay all of our fears of determinism to rest:

> For there remains the question: Who, or what, is responsible for this deeper self? . . . No matter how many levels of the deep self we posit, there will still, in any individual case, be a last level—a deepest self about whom the question "What governs it?" will arise, problematic as ever. . . . Though I can step back from the values my parents and teachers have given me and ask whether these are the values I really want, the "I" that steps back will itself be the product of the parents and teachers I'm questioning. (1987, 377–78)

Wolf notes too that the falsity of determinism is of no help here, since even "if my deepest self is not determined by something external to myself, it will still not be determined by *me*. . . . Whether there is a complete explanation of my origin or no explanation at all, *I* am not, in any case, responsible for my existence; I am not in control of my deepest self" (378). Wolf appeals here to the intuitive plausibility of something like the TNR principle in her criticism of the deep self view.

Frankfurt anticipates worries like these and responds by claiming that human beings can identify *decisively* with a first-order desire and thus have their commitments redound through the potentially infinite series of higher orders desires. At this point, they will not care about the origin of their deepest self, so great is their commitment to their desires (or values). According to Wolf, however, this capacity for decisive commitment is still not enough for moral responsibility. To demonstrate this, she presents a counterexample to the deep self view featuring JoJo, the son of the evil sadistic dictator Jo the First. Jo the First has trained JoJo from early childhood to value arbitrary expressions of cruelty such as executing and torturing his subjects on the basis of mere whim. JoJo understandably sees his father as a role model and acquires a fully authentic deep self that values and endorses cruel behavior as well. Wolf writes: "When he steps back and asks, "Do I really want to be this sort of person?" his answer is resoundingly "Yes," for this way of life expresses a crazy sort of power that forms part of his deepest ideal" (1987, 379).

JoJo, then, meets Frankfurt's and Watson's conditions for morally responsible behavior. Deep self views regard JoJo as no less blameworthy than someone who was brought up in a caring and morally conventional environment. But according to Wolf,

> . . . in light of JoJo's heritage and upbringing, it is dubious at best that he should be regarded as responsible for what he does. It is unclear whether anyone with a childhood such as his could have developed into anything but the twisted perverse sort of person that he has become. (1987, 379–80)

This counterexample leads Wolf to add another condition to the deep self view: *the condition of sanity* or the ability to understand the difference between right and wrong action. Wolf proposes that we are responsible for our actions just in case the actions are a reflection of our authentic selves (the deep self condition) *and* we have the capacity to know right from wrong (the sanity condition). She calls this position the "sane deep self view." According to Wolf, the sane deep self view offers a way of explaining why JoJo is not responsible for his actions "without throwing our own responsibility into doubt (382)." She believes her view provides an account "of why victims of deprived childhoods or misguided societies are not responsible for their actions, without implying that we are not responsible for ours (383)."

The final step in Wolf's argument is to show that the criticism she raised against the deep self view will not apply equally well to her own theory. After all, the most loving childhood and exemplary moral education imaginable do not make us self-determined in the ultimate sense. Sane people—in Wolf's sense—do not create themselves *ex nihilo* any more than JoJo does. According to Wolf, however, once we have the capacity to tell right from wrong, the absence of control at the deepest level should no longer upset us:

> Being sane, we are able to understand and evaluate our characters in a reasonable way, to notice what there is reason to hold on to, what there is reason to eliminate, and what, from a rational standpoint, we may retain or get rid of as we please. Being able to govern our superficial selves by our deep selves, then, we are able to change the things we find there is reason to change. This being so, it seems that although we may not be *metaphysically* responsible for ourselves—for we did not create ourselves from nothing—we are *morally* responsible for our selves, for we are able to understand and appreciate right and wrong, and to change our characters and our actions accordingly. (1987, 384–85)

Wolf's critique of the deep self view and her defense of the sane deep self view relies on the plausibility of two premises, both of which require intuitive agreement. First, we need to share the (controversial) intuition that JoJo is not morally responsible for his cruel behavior because of how he was raised. Second, we must find it intuitively plausible that the addition of the sanity requirement alleviates worries about the lack of ultimate self-determination, and thereby provides the deep self view with sufficient conditions for moral responsibility. And of course, to argue against Wolf's theory one must devise an intuitively plausible counterexample or run a generalization argument like Pereboom's. The cycle continues.

STRAWSONIAN COMPATIBILISM

A different kind of compatibilist theory is developed in P. F. Strawson's groundbreaking essay "Freedom and Resentment." Strawson (2003) seeks to ground attributions of moral responsibility within our blaming and praising practices and, most importantly, within the "participant reactive attitudes" we experience towards other human beings. According to Strawson, these practices and attitudes give us all the justification we need for believing ourselves and others to be free and morally responsible. The general framework of these attitudes and their accompanying beliefs "neither calls for, nor permits, external 'rational' justification" (Strawson 2003, 91).

Since Strawson eschews the search for a rational justification of moral responsibility assignments, his theory does not appeal to intuition in the straightforward manner of Wolf, Frankfurt, Van Inwagen, and Pereboom. Critics, however, have raised concerns about the adequacy of his account. Strawson, they claim, blurs the line between *being* responsible and *being held* responsible.[7] The mere fact that we feel resentment towards someone does not entail that they are blameworthy. It seems possible that an entire society might be misguided about the appropriateness of resentment in certain cases (McKenna and Russell, forthcoming) or in all cases (Russell 1992). Strawson's refusal to allow external criticism of the framework seems to make this state of affairs conceptually impossible. And here is where intuition comes into play. When critics accuse Strawson of minimizing or obliterating the gap between being held responsible and being responsible, they point to an intuitively plausible distinction that must be respected. Strawson, it seems, must also appeal to our intuitions about the concept of responsibility in order to reply.

Some philosophers, such as R. J. Wallace (1998), have sought to remedy the defect in Strawson's theory by bringing normative considerations into the framework. Wallace argues that people are morally responsible when they are *appropriate* targets of the reactive attitudes, when it is *fair* to hold them morally responsible. Wallace is thus able to preserve the distinction between being held responsible and being responsible. People can be resented but not blameworthy when they are not appropriate targets of resentment, when it is not fair to see them as blameworthy. Wallace's modification does indeed remedy the defect in Strawson's position, but it does not aid the cause of an intuition-free approach to moral responsibility. In order to determine when it is fair or appropriate to resent and blame people, we have to consult our intuitions about fairness or appropriateness.

Even the reactive attitudes themselves are sensitive to our intuitions about when they are appropriate. This point can be illustrated by an example of Strawson's:

> If someone treads on my hand accidentally, while trying to help me, the pain may be no less acute than if he treads on it in contemptuous disregard of my existence or with a malevolent wish to injure me. But I shall generally feel in

the second case a kind and degree of resentment that I shall not feel in the first. (2003, 76)

Suppose, however, as sometimes occurs, the resentment does not go away, perhaps due to the intensity of the pain. I may still be grumbling about what a clumsy idiot the person is until my wife appeals to me to relax, saying that it was an accident. She is appealing to my intuitive sense of appropriateness and in doing so may contribute to the resentment subsiding. A factor that diminishes my resentment, then, is my intuition that one shouldn't blame and resent people for accidental behavior. Indeed, Strawson accepts that within the framework of our attitudes, there is room for modification, redirection, criticism, and justification. And these "internal" revisions, modifications, and criticisms seem connected to our intuitions about whether an attitude is appropriate under the circumstances. As Strawson notes, we find it intuitively plausible to take the objective attitude towards the mentally ill, and therefore we try to soften our visceral feelings of anger and resentment. Strawson's theory encourages this kind of internal appeal to our all-things-considered intuitions about the appropriateness of blame and praise.

A final point on Strawson is this. Even if it turned out that Strawson's theory was adequate and lacked an essential appeal to intuition, it would in a significant sense make the relativistic position at the heart of this book *easier* to defend. As I will argue in subsequent chapters, blaming and praising practices vary tremendously across cultures and throughout history, as do the kinds of situations that trigger resentment (and intuitions about the appropriateness of resentment). The nature of these differences would make it impossible to defend universal judgments about the conditions for moral responsibility on Strawson's account. It may be that Strawson would welcome this relativistic implication of his theory, in which case my thesis might be seen as consistent with his position. But since there is no discussion of variation in the reactive attitudes in Strawson's work, it is more likely his theory had universalist pretentions.

MUST THEORIES OF RESPONSIBILITY APPEAL TO INTUITION?

Thus far, I have sought to show that leading theories of responsibility—both compatibilist and incompatibilist—appeal to intuitions about general principles and particular cases for justification. It seems crucial, then, to learn more about the intuitions that determine the success or failure of these theories. One cannot base an argument on the intuitiveness of a premise and at the same time be indifferent to the intuitions of the people to whom the theory is applied. And if one's theory is meant to apply universally, then it would seem that the theory should capture certain universal intuitions, or at least intuitions that would be shared universally under more ideal conditions of rationality.

One might of course concede that leading theories contain this appeal to intuition and reply, "So much the worse for the those theories—moral responsibility 'done right' will not involve such an appeal." But one would then have to give a sense of what this intuition-free approach to establishing the conditions of responsibility would look like—and this is a difficult task. *A priori* approaches that attempt to conceptually link moral responsibility to necessary and sufficient conditions seem doomed to failure. Human beings competently employ the concept of moral responsibility while at the same time disagreeing about conditions of its application. It is not at all clear how one might go about defending something like the sanity condition without appealing to intuition somewhere along the line. Of course one might simply *insist* that sanity is part of the concept of moral responsibility and therefore that theories without the sanity condition contradict themselves or fail to grasp the concept. But this position is untenable. The claim "I know JoJo was unable to know the difference between right and wrong, but he is nevertheless morally responsible for all his cruel actions" is completely intelligible. The speaker is simply stating that JoJo deserves blame for his actions, regardless of his moral upbringing. You might disagree, but in doing so, you would be making a substantive claim about the inappropriateness or injustice of blaming Jojo. You would not be appealing to the *definition* of desert but rather to the intuitively plausible conditions that make its assignment just or appropriate.

Even the most "self-evident" condition, such as a basic control condition, is difficult to support on *a priori* grounds. Throughout history human beings have regularly employed the concept of moral responsibility (in the desert-entailing sense) in cases where control was absent. This is evident even in the Western tradition. A common interpretation of the doctrine of original sin, for example, is that human beings deserve punishment for the actions of Adam and Eve. And Martin Luther explicitly defends the view that human beings can deserve damnation even though they do not control their sinful nature. You may find this wildly counterintuitive, but there does not appear to be any contradiction lurking in this description of moral responsibility.[8] It seems that the concept of desert does not conceptually involve anything like a recognizable control condition. And the same is certainly true for the more sophisticated and hotly contested conditions (such as sanity, indeterministic deliberation, and self-determination) that characterize the contemporary debate. Finally, note that these remarks apply equally well to those who see the conditions of responsibility as part of the concept of responsibility. For they need to appeal to intuitions in order to justify their claim to have identified the true concept of moral responsibility.

Another option is to try to ground one's theory of responsibility on *a posteriori* grounds. One might, for example, attempt to justify conditions of moral responsibility by appeal to their utility or to the degree to which they promote flourishing. This strategy is analogous to the straightforward reductionistic approach adopted by utilitarians in metaethics. The criticisms of this kind of naturalism are well known, and the approach is, if anything, less plausible in the case of moral responsibility because of its association with a non-consequentialist notion of desert. A version of the open question argument can show that there is no essential connection between desert and utility: "I know that blaming [punishing] Bob will bring about the best consequences, but does Bob really deserve blame [punishment]?" is not only a perfectly intelligible question, but also one that we commonly ask ourselves when engaging in these practices.

A more promising approach might be a non-reductionist form of naturalism analogous to metaethical theories developed by "Cornell realists" such as Brink (1984, 1989), Boyd (1988), and Sturgeon and Copp (2005). Such theories develop functionalist accounts of moral values; moral properties like right, good, and bad supervene on natural properties but are not reducible to them. Actions may be morally right, for example, because of the causal role they play in promoting and maintaining human flourishing (Brink 1984). In response to the objection that this is not "what we mean" by morally right, they appeal to the causal theory of reference. Loeb (1998) provides a lucid description of this strategy:

According to the causal theory, reference is not fixed by beliefs alone, but by an appropriate causal relationship between people's use of a term and an object or property in the world. Instead of referring to whatever it is that satisfies some preconceived definition, words refer to whatever entities or properties actually casually regulate their use. . . . Moral terms such as "good" and "right" refer if and only if people's use of these terms is casually regulated by real entities or properties. If it is, then even if we disagree with one another about the nature of goodness, or about which things are good, we are all still referring to goodness. (Loeb, 1998, 293–94)

One could imagine a similar strategy applied to the free will and moral responsibility debate. The property "blameworthiness" would be identified by real natural properties that causally regulated its use. Indeed, P. F. Strawson might have availed himself of this approach to fend off the objection that he conflated "held responsible" with "being responsible." Strawson might have replied that real natural feelings of resentment and gratitude causally regulate our use of terms associated with responsibility, and that it is this that allows us to identify its conditions. Since it is a matter of natural fact that resentment is not diminished by acceptance of the thesis of determinism, we know that determinism is compatible with blameworthiness—and this is true even if we have theoretical beliefs about their incompatibility.

The non-reductionist elements of these theories make it harder to predict the extent to which they are threatened by the existence of cross-cultural disagreement. As far as I know, no philosopher in the free will debate has developed a comprehensive theory of moral responsibility along Cornell realist lines. (Manuel Vargas, in a series of papers, has laid the groundwork for such a theory, but has yet to provide the details.[9]) Since my challenge is empirical in nature, it is best directed at actual theories of moral responsibility rather than potential ones. As noted above, however, I do not think the Strawsonian approach (even with the help of the causal theory) can work as a defense of *universalist* theories of moral responsibility, since there is so much variation in the reactive attitudes themselves. Even if a Strawsonian model did successfully answer the compatibility question, it would not offer a set of universally applicable necessary and sufficient conditions for moral responsibility. In other words, such a theory might establish the truth of compatibilism, but it could not establish *which* of the many compatibilist theories were correct.[10] I suspect that the variation described in the following chapters would undermine other non-reductionist or functionalist models—because responsibility norms and attitudes have different functions, depending on the social structure and physical environment of the society in which the operate. But until the details of such a model are provided, I can only speculate.

Metaskepticism and Skeptical Challenges to Moral Realism

By now it should be clear that my strategy for undermining universalist theories of moral responsibility bears a strong resemblance to arguments from disagreement in the metaethics literature that seek to undermine metaethical realism (e.g., Mackie, 1977; Loeb, 1998; Doris and Plakias 2008). But there are some important differences as well. I have noted that philosophers working on free will and moral responsibility proceed almost exclusively by appealing to intuitions about principles and cases, and then developing theories to accommodate those intuitions. The metaethical literature features a far more diverse set of methodologies for defending moral realism. When these methods lead to fully-developed realist or universalist theories, arguments from disagreement in metaethics must take them into account. Indeed, this is precisely what philosophers like Loeb (1998) have done. However, since theories of moral responsibility are intuition driven, the focus of my challenge concerns variation in these intuitions. If philosophers develop other methods for defending universalist theories of responsibility, I will have to adjust my methods accordingly.

Another related difference between the debates in metaethics and moral responsibility is that metaethical literature features an enormous number of articles and books that focus on the issue of disagreement. Indeed, some of the new methodologies in metaethics have been developed in part to deal with that challenge. By contrast there is not, as far as I know, a single article or book published in the last fifty years that addresses the challenge of disagreement in the free will and moral responsibility debate.[11] (Bernard Williams's excellent book *Shame and Necessity* may be an exception, but it is not specifically directed at the free will problem.) One of my goals in developing a detailed version of such a challenge is to encourage philosophers working on responsibility to grapple with the problem of disagreement—as moral realists of all stripes (intuitionists, rationalists, and naturalists) have done in the metaethical literature. (See e.g., Audi 2007, Brink 1984, Boyd 1988, Smith 1994).

One might object that this division of labor is entirely appropriate. For if metaethical realists can answer the challenge of disagreement and thereby establish the existence of moral facts, the latter will include facts about the conditions for moral responsibility. But this is a mistake. The success of my challenge is not dependent on the success of broader metaethical challenges to moral realism for the simple reason that my challenge relies on a smaller set of empirical claims. Arguments from disagreement in metaethics attempt to establish a more sweeping and ambitious conclusion than the one I defend in this book. Metaethical skeptics or relativists conclude that there are no universally applicable moral facts. My challenge asserts only that there are no universal facts about the conditions of moral responsibility. Certain areas of morality may admit of a realist treatment, while others may not. It is possible that Audi's form of intuitionism, for example, can vindicate realism about prima facie duties, but not realism about the existence of virtues and vices. There might be agreement under ideal conditions of rationality about certain moral questions (the wrongness of causing unnecessary suffering, say), but not others (whether it is permissible to sacrifice one life to save five). In these cases, the proper metaethical conclusion might then be what Doris and Plakias (2008) term a "patchy moral realism."[12] My metaskeptical challenge, however, is only affected if the patches of moral truth cover questions about moral responsibility. For the same reason, the reader should not assume that my position commits me to a broader form of moral relativism. It is entirely possible that metaskepticism about moral responsibility is true, but skepticism or relativism about moral facts in general is not. In chapter 2, for example, I describe the practice of honor killings as support for the view that certain cultures place little emphasis on a control condition for moral responsibility. At the same time, I condemn the practice of honor killings itself. One might think that this pair of attitudes is inconsistent, but it is not. The truth of metaskepticism about moral responsibility does not entail the truth of relativism about the wrongness of killing women suspected of having extramarital relations. If it is a fact that honor killings are wrong, this fact will not have anything to do with facts about the conditions of moral responsibility. The crucial point here is that arguments from disagreement do not stand or fall together. It all depends on the values in question and the nature of the disagreement.[13]

CONCLUSION

My primary goals in this chapter have been to show how leading theories of moral responsibility appeal to intuitions for justification, and then to indicate how these appeals commit the theories to certain assumptions about the universality of these intuitions. In other words, I have tried to show that the claim "I don't care about people's intuitions, I want to know the *truth* about moral responsibility" is untenable. It is precisely by appealing to the intuitions of their audience that philosophers have attempted to describe the truth about moral responsibility. One might reply at this point, "OK, what I meant was that I don't care about the *pre-reflective* intuitions of people who haven't given the issue of moral responsibility any thought. I care about the intuitions of *experts*. I care about the intuitions of philosophers who have devoted a good portion of their lives to addressing this difficult problem." I address this kind of reply in great detail in chapter 4. For now, I would point out that this response ignores the possibility that philosophical theorizing can have a *corrupting influence* on our intuitions as well. Our intuitions might be biased in favor of theories we have spent much of our careers developing.[14] Moreover, even if we concede that the intuitions of philosophers are more reliable than those of "common folk," we cannot assume that these intuitions are uniform among the experts. It could be that equally reflective, intelligent, and rational people in India, Japan, Albania, and inner city Baltimore have radically different starting intuitions and consequently would arrive at different but equally rational considered judgments. The next important question, then, is whether there is such variation in considered judgments. The only way to find out is to look at the evidence, and that is the task of the next three chapters.

CHAPTER TWO

Moral Responsibility and the Culture of Honor

Anthony James has occupied some of the toughest corners of Northeast Washington, D.C. He is also the author of seven books, and has dreams of becoming a full-time author and getting out of "the game" (drug-dealing, violence, prison-time). *Washington Post* writer Kevin Merida says the following about James:

> Every time his mind inches toward embracing the legitimate world's notion of fairness and justice, something happens that shakes him up. And then his mind is back in the streets. On Dec. 2, his half brother, 43-year-old Tracy U. Richardson, was stabbed to death in a fight behind a liquor store in the Eastover Shopping Center on Indian Head Highway near the District line. An Oxon Hill man, 50-year-old Eddie D. Roberson, turned himself in and was charged with first-degree murder.
>
> "I would have rather him stayed on the street—and get some street justice . . . I'm very upset that I can't do nothing about it," A. J. says. "I'm very upset that this dude took

the sucker way out and turned himself in. I'm mad and angry." (Merida 2006).

Although the murderer would likely spend his life in jail as punishment for the crime, A. J. finds the outcome unsatisfying. Eddie D. Roberson is not going to get what he deserves.

• • •

In present day Montenegro, homicidal feuds are common and can be triggered by a single insult or argument. After a first killing, members of the victim's group consider a retaliation murder not only morally permissible but *morally necessary*. The target does not have to be the original murderer or even a relative; it is considered appropriate to kill any member of the offender's group, no matter what their connection to the offense or the offender (Boehm 1984).

• • •

The chieftain Hrafnkels, star of the medieval Icelandic saga *Hrafnkels,* is ambushed at his farm. A rival named Sam tortures Hrafnkels and steals his farm and chieftaincy. Hrafnkels moves east and does not retaliate for six years, suffering the mockery of a servant woman washing clothes by a stream: "The old proverb is very true," she says, "a man gets more cowardly as he ages." Goaded by the woman, he finally retaliates. But his target is not Sam, the man who tortured him and led the ambush on the farm. Rather, it is Sam's brother Eyvind, who has returned to Iceland after being away for seven years. Living abroad has raised Eyvind's status; he is considered "greater than chieftains." Hrafnkels kills Eyvind and reclaims his farm. When Sam appeals to his patrons to prosecute Hrafnkels for murdering his brother, they refuse, claiming that the revenge was justified. Eyvind was a "greater man" than Sam, and was therefore a suitable target for retaliation. Even though he left Iceland more than one year before the ambush and had nothing to do with its planning or execution, his kinship with Sam, and his high status, made him liable for the offense.[1]

• • •

Agamemnon is playing against a stacked deck. He is a member of the house of Atreus, which the Gods have cursed because of the actions of Agamemnon's great-grandfather Tantalus. During the Trojan War, Zeus sends *Ate* (extreme emotion) upon Agamemnon, overwhelming his better judgment and causing him to start a disastrous quarrel with Achilles. The quarrel leads to many deaths, and the other warriors hold Agamemnon responsible in spite of his lack of control. Agamemnon himself deems it necessary to compensate Achilles for having provoked him. But this is only the beginning of Agamemnon's terrible moral luck. Later, in order to fulfill the will of Zeus and attack Troy, he has no choice but to sacrifice his daughter to appease the Goddess Artemis. Once again, Zeus sends *Ate* upon him to hasten the event. Nevertheless, Agamemnon is held responsible by his wife, Clytemnestra, who kills him in a bathtub when he returns home.

• • •

Each of these stories illustrates attitudes about responsibility and justice that do not cohere with any contemporary philosophical theory in the literature. In the first, a man would seem to be getting his just deserts for committing a terrible crime, but the victim's relative is unsatisfied because the punishment comes from a third party. (Justice on Capitol Hill is quite different from the justice of Brentwood in Northeast D.C., less than

four miles away.) In the three subsequent stories, people who
fail to meet both incompatibilist and compatibilist criteria for
morally responsible behavior are thought to be fair targets of
blame or punishment. Separated by thousands of miles and
thousands of years, these characters have one thing in common:
they belong to groups that anthropologists and cultural psychologists have termed "honor cultures." The goal of this chapter is examine the differences between the perspectives of honor
cultures and non-honor cultures towards responsibility and
punishment.[2] I begin by examining the origins of retributive attitudes and of behavior in general. I then examine the different
functions that retributive norms have in honor and non-honor
cultures. Finally, I show how the different functions may give
rise to different beliefs about the conditions for moral responsibility and just punishment.

WHY ARE WE RETRIBUTIVE?

Every known culture features retribution in some form, as well as
norms and beliefs that govern retributive behavior. Yet retributive behavior is in a certain sense irrational.[3] Retaliation cannot
undo the harm caused by the offense, and it often comes with significant cost and risk. Why then is retribution so prevalent? One
common explanation is that retributive attitudes and dispositions are fitness enhancing. Evolutionary theorists since Darwin
have argued that certain emotions and attitudes have been naturally selected to motivate behavior that improves social coordi-
nation. These emotions are especially valuable for motivating actions that go against our immediate self-interest but that yield
long-term reproductive or material advantages. Trivers (1971)
describes the role of retributive emotions in motivating reciprocal altruistic behavior, which enhances the adaptive functioning

of individuals. Frank (1988) describes certain problems—he calls them "commitment problems"—that cannot be solved by rational action. To solve such problems we have instead to commit ourselves to behave in ways that are contrary to our immediate self-interest. Frank develops what he calls the "commitment model," which "is shorthand for the notion that seemingly irrational behavior is sometimes explained by emotional predispositions that help solve commitment problems (Frank 1988, *x*)." Emotions like anger, outrage, and guilt serve as "commitment devices," psychological mechanisms designed to counteract the allure of immediate self-interest in favor of long-term gains. More recently, Richerson and Boyd (2005) have argued that while reciprocal altruism and Frank's theory are part of the story, they cannot fully explain human cooperation in large groups where free-riding is more difficult to detect. They have developed models suggesting that "altruistic punishment"—a willingness to punish non-cooperators at a cost to the punisher—can stabilize cooperative norms in such groups. Fehr and Gachter (2002) and Fehr and Fischbacher (2004) have provided empirical support for these models, and have also illustrated the role of retributive emotions in motivating altruistic punishment.[4] Although the above evolutionary models differ in their details, they all agree that retributive emotions have evolved as a means of motivating human cooperation.

RETRIBUTION AND MORAL RESPONSIBILITY

One may well ask what all this has to do with beliefs about responsibility and desert. Indeed, the authors cited above do not discuss any such beliefs. I have argued, however (Sommers 2007b), that in order to function properly, retributive emotions must be tied to beliefs about moral responsibility. The argument

is as follows. Human beings are creatures of high cognitive sophistication: unlike our early hominid and primate ancestors,
we can question the rationality of our emotions. By this I mean
that we can question (1) whether or not a particular emotion
and the accompanying behavior serves our short-term material
self-interests; and (2) whether or not the emotion makes sense;
i.e., whether it is consistent with other beliefs we hold to be true.
If we find an emotion to be irrational in either sense (but especially the first sense), we are motivated to resist performing the
act that accompanies the emotion. To be sure, we are not always
successful in that attempt. But it is plausible that the link between the emotion and the accompanying behavior would be
undermined *to some degree* by our increased cognitive sophistication. Rational self-interest erodes the link and prevents the
retributive attitude from doing its adaptive work.

This creates an adaptive problem. Retributive behavior is still
fitness-enhancing because of its role in improving social coordi-
nation; but increased cognitive sophistication—which emerged
for other reasons—makes it less likely that the individual will
behave retributively. Human beings therefore require something else to offset the dampening effect of our increased rational capacities. This "something else," I have argued, has taken
the form of norms and beliefs about responsibility.[5]

We can see this belief in desert-based responsibility in action
by referring to an example Robert Frank uses to illustrate his
commitment model. Jones has a $200 leather briefcase that
Smith wants to steal. If Smith steals it, Jones will have to go to
court to recover it and force Smith to go to jail for sixty days. But
the day in court will cost Jones $300 in lost earnings, not to
mention the tedium of a court trial. Since this is more than the
briefcase is worth, it is clearly not in Jones's material self-interest

to press charges. The problem, of course, is that if Smith *knows* that Jones is going to be rational in this way, then he can steal the briefcase with impunity. There's no risk. *But*, Frank writes:

> Suppose that Jones is *not* a pure rationalist; that if Smith steals his briefcase, he will become outraged, and think nothing of losing a day's earnings, or even a week's, in order to *see justice done*. If Smith knows Jones will be driven by emotion, not reason, he will let the briefcase be. If people *expect* us to respond irrationally to the theft of our property, we will seldom *need* to, because it will not be in their interests to steal it. Being predisposed to respond *irrationally* serves much better here than being guided only by material self-interest.[6]

Reading this passage, one might get the impression that outrage alone would be sufficient to predispose Jones to act "irrationally." Frank makes no explicit reference here to any beliefs about moral responsibility or free will. But the belief is there, implicit in the remark about Jones's need to see "justice done." This seems equivalent to the belief that Smith deserves blame and punishment for stealing the briefcase, that he would not receive his just deserts if Jones did not press charges. The belief then that other human beings deserve blame or punishment accompanies attitudes like outrage and plays a role in motivating adaptive behavior. It helps to make the attitude rational and therefore fortifies the link between attitude and adaptive behavior.

Different Norms for Different Cultures

According to this account, retributive behavior and beliefs about moral responsibility are human universals. Where then is the variation? It emerges, I will argue, because retributive norms serve different functions depending upon a society's ecology and social structure. In the following section ("The Function of Retributive Forms in Honor Cultures"), I will show how these different functions result in different attitudes and beliefs about the conditions of moral responsibility. Consequently, while retributive attitudes and concepts of blame and punishment are indeed human universals, there is significant variation in the conditions for their application.

I begin with two passages that illustrate the different ways in which retributive beliefs and attitudes can manifest in honor cultures and non-honor cultures (or "institutionalized cultures," as I will often call them.)[7] In the first, Busquet describes the disgrace that befell persons in the Corsican honor culture who failed to avenge a wrong in a timely fashion:

> Whoever hesitates to revenge himself, said Gregorovius in 1854, is the target of the whisperings of his relatives and the insults of strangers, who reproach him publicly for his cowardice. In Corsica, the man who has not avenged his father, an assassinated relative or a deceived daughter can *no longer appear in public.* Nobody speaks to him; he has to remain silent. (Busquet 1920, 357–58)

The second passage is from Immanuel Kant's *Metaphysics of Morals*:

> But whoever has committed murder, must die. There is, in this case, no juridical substitute or surrogate, that can be given or taken for the satisfaction of justice. . . . Even if a civil society resolved to dissolve itself with the consent of all its members—as might be supposed in the case of a

people inhabiting an island resolving to separate and scatter themselves throughout the whole world—the last murderer lying in prison ought to be executed before the resolution was carried out. This ought to be done in order that every one may realize the desert of his deeds, and that blood-guiltiness may not remain upon the people; for otherwise they might all be regarded as participators in the murder as a public violation of justice. (Kant 1996 [1790], 158)

The first difference between the two perspectives concerns where the normative focus is placed after the offense. In Busquet's description, the focus is on the offended party, on how he ought to respond to the insult and on what happens to him if he fails to respond appropriately. Kant, by contrast, places the focus on the offender—on how he ought to be punished lest the whole of society become accomplices in the "public violation of justice." There is no mention of who should do the punishing.

Now let us look at the environments of these two types of cultures. Nisbett and Cohen (1996) attribute the following features to honor cultures:

1. Cooperation usually occurs within tight-knit groups and among kin. There is relatively little cooperation among strangers.
2. Protection of scarce resources is crucial to survival. One occasion of theft can result in loss of the entire wealth of a family or individual.
3. Attempts to raid or steal the property of others are common.
4. There is little or no protection from the State—the culture is relatively lawless.

The authors maintain that these characteristics are typical of herding and frontier societies. But they note that they may be present in inner city gang life, tribal societies, outlaw and mafia cultures, and other types of environments as well.

The social and economic structure of institutionalized cultures has a quite different set of features and ecology:

1. The economy relies heavily on cooperation and features anonymous interactions and cooperative ventures among relative strangers.
2. The rewards of raids or thefts are not very high, and so protection of resources is not of paramount importance. A single theft cannot cause an individual or family to lose their entire wealth.
3. Discouraging free-riding and cheating is still important, but more for the interests of the group than for any particular individual.
4. There exists some kind of institutional body that governs and enforces norms about cooperation and criminal behavior.

Nisbett and Cohen claim that this type of culture is typical of relatively affluent and stable societies in the West, and of most agriculturally-based communities as well.

THE FUNCTION OF RETRIBUTIVE NORMS IN HONOR CULTURES

Retributive feelings, beliefs, and behavior have important and importantly different functions in both types of cultural environments. In honor cultures, retribution serves primarily as a deterrent to offenses directed at the individual and his family. If you are known as someone who is outraged at the slightest insult—a hair-trigger retaliator who will risk life and limb to punish even the mildest transgressions—potential offenders are far less likely to take advantage of you. Acting according to this disposition will come at great risk, but the risk is outweighed by the future benefits of not having your property, wealth, and livelihood destroyed by a single offense. Norms about honor bridge the gap between an individual's short-term self-interest and the *group's* long-term interest in security and defense against attack (Salzman 2008). Thus, following cultural group selection models such as Richerson and Boyd's, one would expect honor norms to develop in lawless environments.

In addition, since there is in such environments no effective centralized form of law enforcement, it is crucial that the offended party be the one doing the retaliating. Third-party punishment can actually damage the interests of the victim, for if punishment is delivered by a third party, the victim can no longer retaliate. He may then acquire the reputation of being a sucker, an easy mark, a punk, someone to take advantage of without undergoing too much risk (since third-party punishment remains rare). Thus, if an individual is attacked, he must avenge the wrong *himself* to avoid this kind of reputation.

If these observations are correct, we should expect the normative focus in honor cultures to be on the offended party and not the offender. And this is exactly what we find. After insults or offenses occur, there is great normative pressure on the insulted person to avenge himself. The passage by Busquet cited above describes the disadvantages and scorn heaped upon anyone who does not retaliate. Think too of the old woman in the saga who scorns Hrafnkels for not avenging the ambush on his farm. And consider the following passage from Hasluck about the Albanian Highlanders:

A man slow to kill his enemy was thought "disgraced" and was described as "low class" and "bad." Among the highlanders he risked finding that other men had contemptuously come to sleep with his wife, his daughter could not marry into a "good" family. If he does, he retains his honor. (1954, 231–32)

Norms about honor are extremely efficient at motivating appropriate retributive behaviors, as they provide short-term incentives to perform acts in the long-term interests of the group and individual. Although there are significant prudential considerations that weigh against retaliation, these considerations are more than offset by burning shame and the immediate fear of disgrace, ostracism, and a decrease in status for oneself and one's family. Those who do not avenge offenses promptly become targets for future offenses, including "contemptuous" attempts to sleep with their wives.

Also, as expected, third-party punishment is shunned in honor cultures. Albanians consider prison—the epitome of third-party punishment—to be a "nuisance, nothing more than a delay. . . . Prison isn't satisfying for the family" (Blumenfeld 2002, 72). Recall the statement made by Anthony James, the D.C. gang-member, after the murderer of his brother turned himself in: "I would have rather him stayed on the street—and get some street justice. . . . I'm very upset that I can't do nothing about it. I'm very upset that this dude took the sucker way out and turned himself in. I'm mad and angry" (Merida 2006). Third-party punishment strips the victim of his opportunity to avenge himself. Since personal retaliation is crucial, one would expect the emergence of norms that discourage third-party punishment and attitudes that find it to be unsatisfying.

The Function of Retributive Norms in Institutionalized Cultures

The function of retribution in "institutionalized cultures," by contrast, is to discourage free-riding behavior in general. Individuals in such cultures are not at risk of losing their wealth and livelihood from one raid or attempted theft, and so projecting the image of a hair-trigger avenger is not critical. It may actually be harmful, since it will encourage unnecessarily risky attempts at revenge. In an institutionalized culture, then, it makes sense for the normative focus to be on the offender rather than on the offended party. What matters is that the offender be punished (to deter him and others from cheating again). Third-party punishment is quite effective for this purpose. The identity of the retaliator not nearly as important.

What kinds of norms would motivate the appropriate set of behaviors here? Norms concerning *individual* moral responsibility and desert would seem to fit the bill. If we think that only offenders deserve punishment (negative retribution) and that it would be *wrong* for them not to be punished (positive retribution), then, again, the link between retributive feelings and the appropriate form of behavior is reinforced. Refer again to the quotation from Kant. There is no mention whatsoever of the victim or of his family. It makes no difference who avenges the wrong, just as long as the transgressor is punished to avoid the "public violation of justice." A prison term would be satisfying to members of institutionalized cultures; all that matters is that the offender gets what he or she deserves. Compare Anthony James's attitude about his brother's murderer to the reaction of relatives of the Oklahoma City bombing victims to Timothy McVeigh's receiving the death penalty. It was expected that it would bring many of them "closure." It was not "the sucker's way out." The families did not protest that they were being cheated of personal retaliation. Indeed, vigilante justice is most often frowned upon in institutionalized cultures. To achieve satisfaction or closure, it is enough to know that McVeigh has received his just deserts.

Of course, a desire to prevent universal injustice is not nearly as strong a motivating factor as the fear of being dishonored or disgraced. But it does not need to be. Third-party or altruistic punishment often comes at little cost to one's own interests. As Boyd, Gintis, et al. (2003) have argued, altruistic punishment can evolve in large groups precisely because the punishment requires little sacrifice on the part of the punishers (so long as defections remain relatively rare). That cost is more than offset by a general aversion to injustice and by the slight thrill of *Schadenfreude* derived from watching cheaters and defectors suffer. Men especially, according to Singer et al. (2006), derive pleasure from watching a defector suffer the consequences of their transgression—even when they themselves are not the ones who were cheated. Experimenters hooked up subjects to fMRI machines and examined their responses when seeing defectors in public goods games receive a shock.

> Both sexes exhibited empathy-related activation in pain-related brain areas . . . towards fair players. However, these empathy-related responses were significantly reduced in males when observing an unfair person receiving pain. This effect was accompanied by increased activation in reward-related areas, correlated with an expressed desire for revenge. (2006, 467)

This slight thrill is in marked contrast to the ecstasy that individuals in honor cultures experience when they get revenge for a personal insult or attack. According to Djilas (1958, 107) vengeance for Corsicans was "our pastures and springs—more beautiful than anyone else's—our family feasts and births. It was the glow in our eyes, the flame in our cheeks, the pounding in our temples . . . ."

DIFFERENCES IN PERSPECTIVES ON RESPONSIBILITY

Summarizing my observations thus far: Honor culture environments require norms of retribution that put pressure on the offended party. It is of the utmost importance for individuals to show potential future offenders that attempted thefts entail monumental risk to their own interests. Norms about honor provide the motivation to retaliate against even minor offenses, often at great cost, so that the hair-trigger image is conveyed. In institutionalized cultures, by contrast, hair-trigger vigilante justice is generally not worth the risk. But it is still necessary to deter free-riding and anti-social behavior, so norms about individual desert and responsibility—which focus on the intrinsic "rightness" of punishing offenders (and only offenders)—typically emerge to motivate individuals to punish at a minor cost to their own interests. In the following sections, I will describe in greater detail the differences between honor cultures and institutionalized cultures in their attitudes and beliefs about responsibility.

RESPONSIBILITY AND CONTROL

Virtually all Western theories of moral responsibility contain a control condition, although the theories differ on what it means for an agent to have the right kind of control over an action. Theories that lack a control condition are referred to as "strict liability" theories, according to which individuals may be blamed or punished whether or not there was intent, *mens rea,* or negligence on the individual's part. Most people in the West regard strict liability approaches as fundamentally unfair, even if they may, for practical reasons, be appropriate under certain circumstances. As Thomas Nagel puts it, "Strict liability may have its legal purposes, but seems irrational as a moral position" (Nagel 1979, 31).

Evidence from cultural anthropology suggests, however, that denying or de-emphasizing the control condition for moral responsibility may only "seem irrational" to people in certain kinds of societies. In many honor cultures, the condition appears to be either de-emphasized or in some cases absent; agents need not have control over an act in order to be deemed fair and morally appropriate targets of blame and retaliation. Consider the practice of collective punishment—retaliation against people who played no part in committing the offence that is to be avenged. The anthropologist Ram Nath Sharma (1997, 377) writes that in most tribal societies, "the punishment given for murder is death, but this punishment may not be given to him who has murdered. In his place, some other member of his family, group, or clan may be killed since the group is collectively responsible for the criminal acts of each of its members." Of the Inuit people's response to the murder of one of their group members, Balicki (1970, 184) notes: "The objective of the revenge party was not just to kill the original murderer but members of his kindred as well. In a sense the members of the kindred shared responsibility of the murder." Finally, recall Boehm's (1984) description of similar norms and practices in his research on the Montenegrin people. According to Boehm, homicidal feuds are common among Montenegro groups. After a first killing, members of the victim's group consider a retaliation murder not only morally permissible but often morally necessary. The target does not have to be the original murderer or even a relative; it is considered appropriate to kill any member of the offender's group, no matter what their connection to the offense or the offender.

Collective responsibility and punishment is something that individuals in non-honor cultures have a difficult time understanding or justifying.[8] Indeed, the instinct of many raised on the values of individualistic Western culture will be to try to explain away these attitudes, to connect them to something else besides responsibility. For example, one might object that the retaliators in cases of collective punishment do not *truly* deem their targets blameworthy or morally responsible. Perhaps the offended parties are trying to punish and hurt the real offender by harming his friends and family. The problem with this explanation is that the attacks occur even when the offender is dead and so cannot himself be affected by the death of a family member. Or maybe the retaliators are trying to send a message to deter future attacks; perhaps they regard non-offending targets much as Americans view civilians in a war with a repressive regime—as "collateral damage," innocent people who are (unfortunately) caught in the crossfire. But while deterrence and other pragmatic goals may be part of the perceived function of these kinds of attacks, they do not seem to be the whole story. When taking revenge on non-offenders, individuals in honor cultures experience the attitudes associated with responsibility attribution—resentment, moral outrage—toward their targets. Retaliation in honor cultures is never described as "collateral damage" or "regrettable but necessary." Members of honor cultures feel no need for consequentialist justifications. More importantly, they almost never express sentiments or beliefs to the effect that the non-offenders are being unjustly punished. The non-offenders are not innocent; they appear to *deserve* their punishment.

It is also crucial to note the ways that norms supporting collective punishment fit within the broader function of retribution in honor cultures. As emphasized by Miller (1997, 2006), collective responsibility norms encourage groups to police themselves, to prevent their members from starting unnecessary feuds that might put the entire group at risk. One might object that this latter function is a sign that there *is* a control condition for responsibility in honor cultures: perhaps the group is being blamed for failing to control one of its members. But how then could one account for the example in the saga described at the opening of this chapter? Hrafnkels avenges himself not on Sam, the offender, but on Sam's brother Eyvind. Eyvind could not have played any role in planning or executing the ambush, nor could he be blamed for failing to keep Sam under control. He had been out of the country for over a year when the offense occurred. The broader point here is that the function of a particular norm or practice is often independent of its perceived justification. Once norms are in place, "people are motivated to comply with them as *ultimate ends*, rather than as a means to other ends" (Stich and Sripada 2006, 285). Although the function of norms sanctioning collective responsibility is in part to motivate self-policing within groups and to deter other groups from future aggression, members of honor cultures do not the regard the norms primarily as means to those ends. The norms and the intuitions that back the norms acquire intrinsic force. In some cases, entire theories of retribution and individual desert are developed to explain and support them.

INTENTION AND MOTIVE

One central aspect of the control condition in Western theories of moral responsibility involves the agent's motives or intentions. On most accounts, in order to be genuinely blameworthy for wrongdoing, the agent must have intended to perform an action or be guilty of some degree of negligence. This condition is illustrated in penal theory by the (quite recent) emergence of *mens rea* or "guilty mind." As you might expect, however, honor cultures do not find the agent's state of mind to be as central for blame and punishment assignments. The anthropologist Joseph Henrich (personal communication) calls it "common knowledge among anthropologists that in most small-scale societies, you can be blamed for actions you don't intend to do." In a similar vein, Sharma writes that "intent is not very important in the consideration of punishment in tribal society" (1997, 376). He tells the story of a Hupa woman who made a fire in order to heat water and wash clothes. A child got caught in the fire and died as a result. Though the death was entirely accidentally, the woman was forced to sacrifice her own son as punishment.

Another illustration is the terrible and almost incomprehensible practice of "honor killing." The term refers to the murder of a woman or girl (usually by a family member) because she has had extramarital or premarital sex, which is regarded as a stain on the family's honor. What makes these cases even more unfathomable from a Western individualist perspective is that the murders occur even when the woman is a victim of rape. The practice then seems not only brutal and cruel but also *bewildering*. Even if you believe that extramarital sex is a mortal crime, how could it possibly be justifiable to punish rape victims? Rape victims clearly do not intend to perform the act. Yet the woman is still judged to be culpable and is therefore an appropriate target of punishment in the eyes of her family and even in the legal system. According to the *Middle East Report* (Spring 1998), "maintaining honor is deemed a woman's responsibility, *whether or not she has been educated about sex or con-*

sented to the act (my italics)." It is true that in some cases the family members view wives and daughters exclusively as property. But in other cases, the victim is a *beloved* daughter or sister. The murderer may be consumed with grief over the act, and yet he seldom repents. This phenomenon becomes a little easier to understand (although, I stress, not to condone[9]) if we imagine that the cultures supporting this behavior do not regard intention or control as a necessary condition for moral responsibility. If that is the case, it becomes almost irrelevant that the victim did not choose, or intend, to have extramarital sex. All that matters is that the act occurred. The idea that it is unjust to punish someone for unintended acts would not resonate as much to members of these cultures.[10] (Of course, I do not believe extramarital sex is a crime, much less a mortal crime, whether or not it is intended. The point is that intention seems not to matter nearly as much for these cultures.)

Again, one's first instinct might be to try to explain away this seeming indifference to the intentions of the women—to claim that something other than responsibility is at work here. (Indeed, I have proposed an alternate hypothesis myself.[11]) It is possible that those who perform such a killing do so not out of any sense that the woman deserves it, but out of a higher duty to rescue the honor of the family. Perhaps the rape is viewed as some kind of terminal and contagious disease. On the other hand, there are cases in which the punishment of the rape victim is not death but lashes administered in accordance with a judge's ruling. These rulings indicate that there is some notion of moral desert at work, although one may argue that the blame stems from some exotic interpretation of the woman's intent. It is also true that there are many people within these cultures who find honor killings barbaric and fight against the practice. Crucially, however, their objections seldom focus on the lack of control or intention of the victim, but rather on the wrongness of killing women for having extramarital sex, whether they intended to or not.

MANIPULATION

Several years ago, I was compelled to watch the movie *Ella Enchanted* with my daughter Eliza. At the beginning of the film, a confused and somewhat neurotic fairy puts an "obedience" spell on Ella, the Cinderella-like heroine, which causes her to do everything that is asked of her, no matter how imprudent or immoral. Her wicked stepsisters discover the spell and force her to do a number of vile and dangerous things against her will. In one scene they order her to tell her best friend that she is no longer allowed to enter the house because of the inferiority of her race. Relunctantly, with tears in her eyes, Ella obeys. The friend, who does not know about the spell, is shocked and deeply hurt. But the intuition of the filmmakers (and most of the audience, I imagine) is that while the action itself is vile, it is unfair to blame Ella for performing it. Every bit of the blame should fall on her wicked sisters, for Ella is only a victim of their manipulation.[12]

Most theories of moral responsibility require that agents be free of overt manipulation in order to be held morally responsible for their acts. Even the relatively permissive theories of the classical compatibilists require that agents not be constrained when performing their actions. This is yet another condition that seems to be de-emphasized in honor cultures. Compare Ella's plight to Agamemnon's as described in dramas by Sophocles and Aeschylus. Agamemnon is compelled to murder his daughter in order to set sail for Troy—which is required by the will of Zeus. For good measure, Zeus sends *Ate* to confound

Agamemnon's wits before he makes the decision. Lloyd-Jones (1962, 192) describes the circumstances as follows:

> Zeus is indeed determined that the fleet must sail; Agamemnon has indeed no choice. But how has Zeus chosen to enforce his will? Not by charging Calchas or some other accredited mouthpiece to inform the king of his decision; but by sending *Ate* to take away his judgment so that he cannot do otherwise. Does it follow that Agamemnon is not held responsible for his action? Certainly not.

In spite of the constraint *and* the manipulation, Clytemnestra and the Chorus (in Aeschylus's version) hold Agamemnon morally responsible for the act.

Nussbaum (1985) notes how difficult it is for classical scholars to make sense of this seemingly irrational attitude about moral responsibility. He cites the German critic Albin Lesky, who writes:

> If one makes a clear logical distinction, of course, one will say: "A man who acts under necessity is not acting voluntarily." But to insist upon logical consistency would mean that we should have to reject considerable parts of Aeschylus' tragedies. . . . In fact, the stumbling-block in the way of any attempt at logical analysis goes much farther. . . . Is not the campaign against Troy a just punishment inflicted on behalf of the highest god, Zeus, who protects the rights of hospitality? Thus, Agamemnon acts on behalf of the god who wills this punishment. And yet the price for this punishment is a terrible guilt, for which the king has to atone with his death. *Here there is no logical consistency.* (Lesky 1966; cited in Nussbaum 1985, 235. My italics)

Lesky's remarks are striking because there is in fact no logical inconsistency whatsoever. Inconsistency would only arise if something like a principle of alternate possibilities were built into the concept of guilt; and clearly (for the Greeks) it was not. The judgment of Agamemnon is not illogical, it is *counterintuitive* from a contemporary Western perspective.

Nussbaum describes an interesting way of resolving the tension. She claims that Agamemnon is judged not for his crimes, but for his emotional response to them. He performs them too clinically, without sufficient reluctance. Consequently, the Chorus and Clytemnestra view him as lacking *virtue* and blame him accordingly.[13] By contrast, someone like Ella is deeply saddened when she insults her friend—the act goes against everything she believes in—and so we acknowledge her virtue and do not blame her in the same way.

This is an attractive reconciliation between Western attitudes about manipulation and the Greek view of Agamemnon's guilt, and it receives some support from a recent experimental study as well. Woolfolk, Doris, et al. (2006) presented subjects with a number of scenarios in which an agent was compelled to perform an immoral action, and they manipulated the degree to which the agent "identified" with the act. Their results show that subjects attributed more responsibility and blameworthiness when the agent identified with the action, even if the agent was unable to do otherwise. They conclude that:

> Cognition involving moral attribution is strongly influenced by extra-causal factors, i.e., factors other than those that are likely to figure in the most careful and thoughtful causal explanation of the behavior in question. One such factor is the evaluative attitudes of the actor; what it is that the actor wants to come about or wants not to come about . . . What causes people to attribute responsibility, to praise

or blame, is to some extent what is believed to be in the
"heart" of the actor and this is so even for actions committed under overwhelmingly coercive or constraining circumstances of "absolute constraint."

Thus one could say of Agamemnon that he is responsible
for the constrained actions because he identified too closely
with them (or did not present sufficient evidence of a *lack* of
identification).

Attractive as it might be, I do not believe this analysis gets to
the heart of Greek attitudes about responsibility. For Zeus has
not only presented Agamemnon with a "Sophie's choice" kind
of dilemma, he has also manipulated Agamemnon's feelings and
attitudes by sending *Ate* to take away his wits. As Lloyd-Jones
points out, this occurs in the *Iliad* as well, when Zeus wants
Agamemnon to start a quarrel with Achilles. If Agamemnon's
emotions are being manipulated to incite him to perform the
action, we cannot say that he identifies with it, at least at the moment when the action is performed. Nussbaum notes that
Agamemnon's son Orestes faces a similar predicament:

> The helpless Orestes, forced by a god's command to kill his
> guilty mother, and far more appropriately reluctant before
> this awful act, must also have his punishment: the mad-
> ness of remorse and pursuit by his mother's furies. (1985,
> 256)

Guilt and responsibility are assigned even when identification is
absent. It seems then that in the Greek honor culture, one could
be responsible and justly punished for fated, constrained, or manipulated actions, whether one identified with the action or not.

One objection commonly raised to examples like this is that
the Greeks simply lacked the concept of a moral responsibility

that requires control. Such a concept requires, the argument goes, a more mature ethical perspective than prevailed at the time. Had they known of the concept, they might well have embraced it. But this is not correct, for it seems that the Greeks were well aware of the idea that manipulation or fate could eliminate responsibility; they simply did not accept it. When Agamemnon causes Achilles to leave the war in the *Iliad*, the result is an untold number of Greek deaths. Achilles and the other Greek generals hold Agamemnon responsible for the unnecessary public insult to Achilles' honor, and, as noted above, Agamemnon himself feels compelled to offer large compensation for his act. But, interestingly, Agamemnon does claim that the whole affair is not his fault:

> But I want each of you to mark my words.
> There is not a Greek here who has not said
> Spiteful things about me. But I am not to blame.
> Zeus is, and Fate, and the Dark Avenger,
> Who put a fit of madness on me, in public,
> The day I robbed Achilles of his prize.
> But what could I do? Gods decide everything.
> Zeus's eldest daughter is the Goddess Ate,
> Who binds everyone, a deadly power.
> *Iliad* XIX: 97–105, Lombardo, trans. 1997, 377.

Agamemnon is clearly trying to excuse himself from blame here by appealing to his lack of control. Fate, Zeus, and Ate made him do it. Starting this fight with Achilles was not his choice, it did not originate in *him*. So how can he be blameworthy? The Greeks, then, were aware of a concept of moral responsibility that required control, and perhaps even some kind of sourcehood. (Maybe source incompatibilism goes back a lot farther than we think!)

This is not an isolated example. Characters in the *Iliad* also attempt to strip glory away from their enemies by appealing to their lack of control. After falling at the hand of Hector, Patroclus gasps, "Brag while you can, Hector. Zeus and Apollo have given you an easy victory this time. . . . It was Fate, and Leto's son, who killed me. You came in third at best (Lombardo 1997, 330 [XVI: 885–90])." Even Achilles' horse Xanthus appeals to this excuse, saying "We are not to blame, but a great God and strong Fate" when Achilles' accuses them of leaving Patroclus to die (Lombardo, 1997, p. 386. [XIX: 438-39]).

These examples show that the Greeks of Homer's time were well aware that one could appeal to a lack of control in order to excuse behavior. At the same time, though, they seem to undermine my claims about cultural differences, in particular my argument that the honor culture of Homeric Greece embraced a concept of moral responsibility that did not require control. But here is the crucial point. Although Homer's heroes are aware that agents may appeal to factors such as God's intervention, Fate, and a general lack of control as an excuse, they do consider these factors to be a *good* excuse. No one ever agrees with the heroes (or the horses) that the agent is excused from blame. It comes across as sour grapes, the bitterness of a vanquished foe, or a contemptible attempt to sidestep one's responsibility for what has occurred. In a sense, using Fate or the will of the Gods as an excuse was the Homeric equivalent of the infamous "Twinkie defense."

RESPONSIBILITY FOR PUBLIC AND PRIVATE ACTIONS

The final kind of variation that I will discuss in this chapter concerns how the public or private nature of an action can affect responsibility. Western theories of moral responsibility tend to focus almost exclusively on the agent and the agent's state of mind, and regard the public vs. private aspect of an action as largely irrelevant.[14] In deep self views, for example, if you commit an offense that is endorsed by a value or a higher order desire, then you are morally responsible for the offense. It makes no difference whether the act is discovered or not. Similarly, you can be praiseworthy and virtuous even when no one else considers you to be so, when no one knows of any virtuous actions that you have performed. It doesn't matter what others think of you, what matters is what you do and how you regard yourself.

This notion of self-esteem as a gauge of personal worth would not pass muster in honor cultures. Indeed, it may be close to incoherent. As virtually all researchers who study such cultures note, honor is there an entirely public matter. Gaining or losing honor without anyone knowing about it is a conceptual impossibility. Miller (1993, 116) writes:

> In an honor-based culture there was no self-respect independent of the respect of others, no private sense of "hey, I'm quite something" unless it was confirmed publicly. Honor was then not just a matter of the individual, it necessarily involved a group, and the group included all those people worthy of competing with you for your honor.

The emphasis on how one is perceived has important implications for moral responsibility in honor cultures. It makes little sense for agents to be praiseworthy for private actions or aspects of their character. Perception is too important, it plays too big of a role in the social lives of groups and individuals. The idea of blameworthiness for undiscovered wrongdoing is difficult to appreciate as well. Salzman (2008, 122) provides a striking example of this perspective in the case of a Bedouin honor killing:

> It was not the sexual misbehavior that led her father and sisters to kill the girl; rather, it was the public accusation. As Ginat (1997, 136) says, "The father did not kill his

daughter when he learned that she had offended the
norm. It was his wife's accusation, made in public . . . that
prompted him to take steps." This circumstance—a public
accusation by an injured party, i.e., one who also loves
honor—appears, according to Ginat (1997, 136, 187, and
passim) as a major element, perhaps almost a *necessary element*, in a murder for sexual misbehavior. Absent such an
accusation, murder rarely if ever takes place. (my italics)

Thus, it appears that among the Bedouins, public discovery of
the wrongdoing is *a necessary condition* for justified punishment. This perspective may also shed further light on why motive and intention are not essentially connected in honor cultures. The key factor is not whether agents wished to perform
the actions; rather it is whether public knowledge of the act will
bring honor or dishonor on the family. Given the supreme importance of perception, such private subjective features of an act
as its causal history are de-emphasized when it comes to assigning moral responsibility. Instead, agents are judged by what *can*
be perceived: the act itself.

A related feature of honor-based systems is that people can
acquire a high reputation as a result of appearance, strength,
and family associations—in other words, for public characteristics over which the agents clearly have no control. One can deserve praise and blame for perceived aspects of one's character
that one cannot help possessing. Russell (2004, 178) writes of
the Christian view that "*moral* merit is concerned solely with
acts of will; i.e., with choosing rightly among *possible* courses of
action. I am not to blame for not composing an opera because I
don't know to do it." But according to the Greek view, one can be
praiseworthy or blameworthy for talents and abilities, virtues
and vices, that do not trace back to choices made over the course

of one's life. (I will discuss this kind of variation further in chapter 3, in the context of distinguishing between shame cultures and guilt cultures.)

CAVEATS AND CONCLUSION

Some caveats are in order. First and most important: the differences I have been describing between honor cultures and non-honor cultures are differences of degree, not of kind. The variation in responsibility perspectives should be regarded as ranging along a continuum. Aspects of one perspective will be present to lesser degrees in the other and vice versa. Responsibility norms and attitudes will also likely vary according to context. The conditions of moral desert in honor culture may, for example, become more stringent in close interpersonal relationships.[15] And strong honor norms may be prevalent under certain circumstances in non-honor cultures.

The strict code governing beanballs in baseball is a prime example. When a pitcher hits the opposing team's player, the opposing pitcher is obligated to retaliate—not against the pitcher himself (impossible with the DH in the American League) but against a player of equal stature to the player that was originally hit. If the pitcher fails to retaliate, he is often shunned by his teammates. This intricate form of collective blame and punishment bears more resemblance to the usages of Saga Iceland than to anything found in Western theories of moral responsibility.

Finally, there is certain to be variation between individuals *within* cultures. One fascinating example is Laura Blumenfeld, a *Washington Post* journalist and the author of a book called *Revenge*. Blumenfeld was a quiet, diminutive Harvard graduate from a middle-class Jewish family on Long Island—about as far from an honor culture as one could get—or so it would seem.

When Blumenfeld was in her twenties, her father visited Israel and was shot by a Palestinian. Blumenfeld then embarked on a decade-long quest to avenge her father's injury. This mission baffled her friends and family. There was no long-term damage, and the shooter was in prison. Even the victim himself was completely satisfied that justice had been carried out. When asked by her friend Rachel to explain her obsession, Blumenfeld was almost too embarrassed to reply. After making Rachel promise not to laugh, Blumenfeld replies: "I wanted to them to know . . ."

> "That you can't shoot your Dad?"
> "No, not that . . . that you can't . . . *you can't fuck with the Blumenfelds!* . . . That there's someone you have to answer to. . . ." (Blumenfeld 2002, 114)

Blumenfeld alone (her father and brother did not participate in her quest) felt that her family had been dishonored by the attack and that the shooter's prison-term was in no way a remedy for the dishonor. This is exactly the type of "honor" norm that I have been describing—one that focuses on the victim and his family.[16] But it comes from a most unlikely source.

The complexity of responsibility norms and the individual differences within cultures are fascinating. But they do not diminish the significance of the systematic cross-cultural variation. Honor cultures and non-honor cultures appear to occupy very different areas of a wide spectrum. Moreover, as I have tried to show, the variation can emerge as a natural response to features of the environments in which these cultures operate—a consideration that I will focus on in much greater detail in chapter 4. My next chapter continues to provide evidence for the systematic diversity of intuitions and attitudes across cultures.

CHAPTER THREE

Shame Cultures, Collectivist Societies, Original Sin, And Pharaoh's Hardened Heart

SHAME CULTURES

In 1944, the U.S. Office of War Information commissioned anthropologist Ruth Benedict to write an analysis of Japanese culture to aid in the war effort. Two years later she published her book *The Chrysanthemum and the Sword* and introduced the controversial distinction between shame cultures and guilt cultures. According to Benedict, in cultures where shame is the dominant emotion, the norms are essentially tied to the perception of one's behavior, character traits, and appearance (just as they are in honor cultures).[1] Guilt cultures, by contrast, focus on the act from the individual's perspective:

> True shame cultures rely on external sanctions for good behavior, not, as true guilt cultures do, on an internalized conviction of sin. . . . [Shame] requires an audience or at least the fantasy of an audience. Guilt does not. In a nation

* Much of the material from this chapter appears in an article published as "The Two Faces of Revenge: Moral Responsibility and the Culture of Honor" in *Biology and Philosophy*, 89 (3). 511–521; it is reproduced here with kind permission of the copyright holder, Springer Science+Business Media.

where honor means living up to one's own picture of oneself, a man may suffer from guilt though no man knows of
his misdeed and a man's feeling of guilt may actually be
relieved by confessing his sin. (Benedict 2005 [1946], 223)

Individuals in guilt cultures respond to internalized demands
from the self, avoiding misdeeds because of their internalized
psychological costs.[2] Individuals in shame cultures refrain from
norm violations because of the social costs they entail. They
may also experience shame for conspicuous events that they did
not intend to bring about, or at times even play a role in bringing about (as illustrated in the response of Koreans to the Virginia Tech massacre). In guilt cultures, these acts are seen as appalling but not something for which non-offenders should feel
guilty.

Benedict has been accused of making too sharp a contrast, of
ignoring subtleties and shadings. But it may be her critics who
are guilty of oversimplifying Benedict's views, for she was well
aware that the shame-guilt distinction was one of degree.[3] This
distinction as it relates to moral responsibility may operate in
the following way: if agents violate norms in a shame culture but
the violation is undiscovered, the agents are less likely to hold
themselves responsible; agents in guilt cultures will likely hold
themselves responsible whether or not the offence is discovered.
A famous example of "guilt culture responsibility" is the character Raskolnikov in *Crime and Punishment*, who feels searing
guilt and a subsequent need to confess to a crime that no one
knows he has committed. A reader in a true shame culture may
find it hard to relate to Raskolnikov's struggle.[4]

In his book *Culture's Consequences*, Hofstede employs a description from E. M. Forster's *A Passage to India* to illustrate
the different motivations of people from these two types of
cultures:

Aziz upheld the proprieties, though he did not invest them with any moral halo, and it was here that he chiefly differed from the Englishman. His conventions were social. There is no harm in deceiving society as long as she does not find you out, *because it is only when she finds you out that you have harmed her.* (Hofstede 2001, 212, my italics)

Forster, according to Hofstede, echoes the common view of sociologists and cultural psychologists that members of shame cultures are less committed to moral absolutes. Moral wrongness, and therefore blameworthiness, is not fully acknowledged until the discovery of the deed. If an act remains undiscovered, there is nothing for the individual to be blameworthy *for.* By the same token, members of shame cultures may feel responsible for a class of actions for which members of guilt cultures would hold themselves blameless: conspicuous harmful acts that are in some sense connected to the individual, but that the individual did not intend to bring about. Recall Kyeyoung Park's observation that Koreans did not merely feel shame for the act of the Virginia Tech killer, they felt *responsible.* They wished to apologize and atone for the act—attitudes and behavior that are intimately connected with feelings of moral responsibility.

Again, these are differences of degree and not kind. Many Americans can identify *to an extent* with the shame experienced by the Koreans. And it is likely that Koreans can appreciate in part why Americans found their reactions so puzzling. Nevertheless, the differences in degree may be significant and therefore have implications for the shame and guilt cultures' intuitions about moral responsibility. The relative emphasis on shame leads East Asians to connect blameworthiness with social disapproval, and also to feel responsible for public acts over which they have little or no control. An increased emphasis on guilt in the West makes it more likely that individuals will hold themselves responsible for both public *and* private misdeeds, but only for those that they played an active role in bringing about.

In the next section, I will outline a more nuanced and complex view of the cultural differences between (broadly speaking) Eastern and Western cultures and explore how these differences relate to moral responsibility and justice.

Individualism and Collectivism

Nowadays when psychologists and sociologists speak about cultural differences between Japan and the U.S.—or more generally between East and West—they are likely to use the term "collectivist societies" for the East and "individualist societies" for the West. (See e.g., Hofstede 2001; Triandis, Bontempo, et al. 1988; Kim and Hakhoe 1994, Markus and Kityana 1991). The foundational treatise for this paradigm is Gert Hofstede's *Culture's Consequences*. Hofstede conducted a study of more than 117,000 IBM employees in sixty-six countries. He found four dimensions of cultural variation: power distance, uncertainty avoidance, individualism, and masculinity. As Kim et al. (1994) note, it is the dimension of individualism that has most captured the interest of cultural psychologists:

> It is considered by many to be a bipolar dimension, with individualism on one end and collectivism on the other. The United States, Canada, and Western European countries were found to be high on the individualist end of this dimension. Asian, Latin American, and African nations were found to be high on the collectivist side. (Kim et al. 1994, 1)

Kim and colleagues go on to describe the different features of each kind of society:

> Individualist societies emphasize "I" consciousness, auto-nomy, emotional independence, individual initiative, right to privacy, pleasure seeking, financial security, need for specific friendship, and [moral] universalism. Collectivist societies, on the other hand, stress "we" conscious-ness, collective identity, emotional dependence, group solidarity, sharing, duties, obligations, need for stable and predetermined friendship, group decision, and [moral] particularism. (Kim et al. 1994, 2)

The two societies also employ different conceptions of the self. The individualist self is regarded as discrete, autonomous, and rational (Triandis, Bontempo, et al. 1988; Markus and Kitayama 1991). There is "a sense of self with a sharp boundary that stops at one's skin and clearly demarcates self from non-self" (Spence 1985, 1288, cited in Kim et al. 1994, 28). The collectivist self, by contrast, is conceived of as contextual, embedded, and situated within certain roles and statuses that make up the group. Clear lines separate groups, but there is a "porous boundary between the individual self and the group to which it belongs. The self is defined in terms of its in-group relationships (Triandis 1995). This view of the self may sound odd to the Western ear, but a great deal of evidence from sociology, anthropology, and cultural psychology suggests that it is prevalent.[5] As Clifford Geertz puts it:

> The Western conception of a person as a bounded, unique, more or less integrated motivational and cognitive uni-verse, a dynamic center of awareness, emotion, judgment, and action organized into a distinctive whole and set con-

trastively both against such wholes and against a social and cultural background is, however incorrigible it may seem to us, a rather peculiar idea within the context of the world's cultures. (Geertz 1973, 48; cited in Hamilton and Sanders 1992, 52–53)

Research indicates that the differing views of the self in collectivist and individualist societies lead to differences in thinking about the conditions for moral responsibility. Most significantly, individualist societies tend to place greater weight on the mental state of the offender than do collectivist societies. Collectivist societies, by contrast, tend to assign more weight to factors relating to role and hierarchy than do individualist societies. As was also the case with honor cultures, beliefs concerning conditions for moral responsibility seem well adapted to the social structure of the societies in which they emerge. This feature of beliefs about moral responsibility plays an important role in my argument, as I will show in the following section and especially in chapter 4.

Japanese and American Perspectives on Responsibility

One striking illustration of the relevant differences comes from a series of studies by Hamilton and Sanders (1981, 1988, 1992) that probe explicitly for responsibility judgments in the United States and Japan. Subjects from Detroit and two Japanese cities—Yokahama and Kanazawa—were given vignettes featuring wrongdoing and asked to assess responsibility and assign punishment. The authors outlined three factors that could influence assignments of responsibility in both Japan and the U.S.:

1. *The deed.* How severe was the harm? What was the agent's mental state? To what degree was the act intentional?

2. *The context.* Was there was a past pattern of wrongful behavior? To what extent was the offender influenced by another person?

3. *The role relationships.* What is the relationship of the offender to the victim?

The authors believed that all of these factors would influence responsibility assignments in both countries. Agents would be held more responsible for acts that showed a high degree of intention on the part of the agent, less responsible when the act was influenced by another person. And offenders who held a higher position in their hierarchical relationship to the victim (boss to employee or mother to child) would be assigned greater responsibility than offenders who were the equals of their victims.

Though Hamilton and Sanders predicted that subjects from both countries would take all of the factors into account, they also predicted systematic variation in the *weight assigned* to each factor when determining overall responsibility. This prediction was confirmed. As expected, Americans placed far more importance on issues relating to the agent's mental state or intentions than did the Japanese. "The actor's state of mind when wrongdoing or harm-doing occurred," the authors reported, "was *approximately twice as important* a determinant of responsibility for Detroiters as it was for Japanese respondents (Hamilton and Sanders 1992, 122). In addition, Japanese subjects were far more sensitive than Americans to the social context in which the offense occurred. They assigned far greater responsibility when the offender was in a position of authority over the victim than when the two were equals. Americans assigned only slightly more responsibility in these cases. The Japanese also tended to take the influence of others into account, assigning considerably less responsibility when influence was present.

American assignments did not decrease when influence was present, except in those cases where the influence came from an authority figure. Finally, Japanese judgments varied a great deal when solidarity (the closeness of the relationship of victim to offender) was manipulated, whereas Americans placed little or no value on solidarity considerations.

It is of course possible that the Japanese are simply less discerning about mental states, about whether or not an act truly reflects the intentions of the offender. But the data do not support this interpretation. The one type of case in which the Japanese did place great weight on mental state factors was when the offender was in a position of authority over the victim. In those cases, the Japanese showed that they understood the intentions of the offender. Thus, it would be surprising if they had failed to do so in other cases. It seems, as the authors note, that the Japanese *make less use of* information about the actor's mental state in determining responsibility, but they do not ignore mental state information. (This is important to recognize, as one common strategy for explaining away such variation is to suggest that one party is unaware of crucial, relevant facts.)

Significantly, the authors did not discover variation alone; they discovered *systematic* variation that was in line with their theoretical models; that is, with their expectation that differences in the social structure of the two countries would correlate to differences in assignments of responsibility:

> In a society where actors are viewed as isolated individuals, information about individual attributes and deeds, especially about the actor's mental state, should be relatively more important in assessing responsibility than in societies where actors are viewed as contextuals. . . . Because another's influence is perceived as both more real and more

legitimate in a contextual culture, Japanese should be more sensitive than Americans to the impact of influence from others on responsibility. (Hamilton and Sanders 1992, 87)

And the results supported the model:

For Americans, information about mental state is particularly salient, and it is relatively resistant to reinterpretation as a function of actors' social roles. For Japanese, information about roles and others' influence is particularly salient. Insofar as all deeds are committed in roles and in context, Americans appear to focus on the deed and resist the reinterpretation that can occur because of role or context; Japanese focus on the context and shift their interpretation of the deed accordingly. (88)

The models derived from this study are in line with the views I outlined above in discussing individualist vs. collectivist conceptions of the self. In collectivist societies, where the boundaries between the individual self and the group are "porous," the intentions of an individual offender should not matter *as much*, and the social context of the offense should matter more when assigning responsibility. In individualist societies, where the self is conceived of as autonomous and discrete "with a sharp boundary that stops at one's skin," social context should be seen as less important than the intentions of the autonomous individual.

The implications of these results are in one sense quite difficult to assess for my thesis. This is because the contemporary philosophical debate has proceeded in large part as though moral responsibility was an all or nothing affair. It is surprisingly difficult to find discussions in the philosophical literature of *degrees* of moral responsibility. Perhaps this is because theories of moral responsibility tend to be framed in terms of necessary and sufficient conditions.[6] Hamilton and Sanders's studies, however, proceeded under the assumption that moral responsibility *is* a degree concept. Subjects were asked to assess the responsibility of the offender on a scale of 1 to 10, and many in both cultures assigned scores in the 3 to 8 range, indicating that they were comfortable with the concept of degrees of responsibility.

What I can say is this. If theories of responsibility cannot accommodate beliefs about degrees of moral responsibility, then they have an even more serious flaw than the one I am aiming to expose. For the theories would in fact capture *no one's* concept of responsibility other than that of a professional philosopher. I suspect, however, that the theories can accommodate a degree view by regarding the capacities required for responsibility as coming in degrees. If this is the case, the Hamilton and Sanders studies are important, for they reveal variation in intuitions about the conditions for moral responsibility. The differences do not (in all cases) concern *what the conditions are*, but rather *how important each of the conditions is* in overall determinations of responsibility. A control condition is not absent from Japanese views of responsibility, but it is considerably deemphasized. And while Americans do not see social influence as *irrelevant* (although it is close to irrelevant when the influence comes from an equal), they do find it to be far less exculpatory than do their Japanese counterparts.

Finally, the differences do not seem to be a result of factual mistakes on the part of one group or the other. Rather, as I continue to emphasize, they arise out of the different social structures, value systems, and views of the self that characterize individualist vs. collectivist societies.

Original Sin and Pharaoh's Hardened Heart

Early religious texts are a rich source of evidence on variation in attitudes towards responsibility. Consider the doctrine of original sin, or "original guilt" as it is often called. As Michael Rea describes it, the doctrine holds that "all human beings . . . are guilty from birth in the eyes of God, and this guilt is a consequence of the first sin of the first man." (Rea 2007, 1) The idea strikes many as obviously unfair. After all, it was Adam who ate the apple, not me. What Adam did was his business—why should I get blamed for it? For centuries theologians have struggled to explain away the apparent injustice of this doctrine. One strategy, originally proposed by Augustine, is to claim that in a real metaphysical sense *we are Adam*. We are unified by our human nature, and so we all committed the act of eating the apple of our own free will. Aquinas develops this response by employing the analogy of a human body—each individual is a part of the body that is the human race. So when Adam sinned, we sinned. Just as our hands suffer the consequences of actions performed by our minds, so we should suffer the consequences of Adam's action. There are examples of even more elaborate metaphysical maneuverings, but all seem unsatisfying—even, at times, to the theologians who propose them. It seems unjust to blame us for an act that occurred long before we were born, one that we played absolutely no role in bringing about.[7]

This problem has two interesting features. The first involves the possibility of justifying the doctrine. Augustine's theory of a unified human nature attempts to address this aspect. Skeptics and agnostics, of course, do not face the problem of justification. They do not believe there was an Adam—and even if there had been, they deny that we would be responsible for his actions. Even for the skeptic, however, there remains a question that must be addressed. How and why did this doctrine emerge as a dominant feature of Christianity? Why did *anyone* think it could be fair of God to blame the whole human race for the actions of the first man in the Garden of Eden? These puzzles only arise, however, if we think that there is and always has been a control condition for moral responsibility. If there was no such condition at the time the doctrine was conceived, there would be nothing unfair about God blaming us for a sin our ancestor committed. The people who thought up "original sin" would have had no way of knowing that the doctrine might lead to thousands of years of theological controversy.

One consideration in favor of this hypothesis is that the God of the Bible seems to blame us all the time for acts over which we had no control. Indeed, one of the thorniest theological problems is how to reconcile free will and personal accountability with God's omnipotence: if God is the ultimate cause of every sin, why isn't he blaming himself rather than the people he has caused to sin? I will not address this much discussed question but rather focus on something that seems even more inconsistent to those who hold to the notion of individualist responsibility: the occasions where God not only serves as the *ultimate* cause of human beings behaving badly, but also as the proximate cause. Just as Zeus manipulated Agamemnon (see chapter 2), the God of the Old Testament will actively manipulate a person's nature so as to cause him to sin —and then punish him for that sin.

Jonathan Edwards (1957) provides an impressive list of such episodes;[8] I will focus on only one, a famous example from Exodus. As the story goes, God summons Moses and tells him to go to the Pharaoh and demand freedom for the Israelites. Pharaoh refuses. God sends Aaron and Moses back to show the Pharaoh a little magic (turning a staff into a snake) and to issue a warning that plagues will follow if he does not comply. Pharaoh refuses again. God starts to get serious and turns the river to blood, killing all the fish. Moses goes back to Pharaoh, but Pharaoh remains obstinate. It is only after ten increasingly grisly plagues (concluding with the death of every Egyptian's first born) that Pharaoh finally relents, devastated at having lost his son.

So far there is nothing here to offend ordinary sensibilities. Pharaoh shows himself to be not merely a cruel tyrant, but also a stubborn and irrational one, who refuses to back down even when it is clear that his people will suffer from his obstinacy. If anyone deserves terrible blame and punishment, it's Pharaoh. But there is a complication. God is both the ultimate and *proximate* cause of Pharaoh's obstinacy. God actively manipulates Pharaoh, hardens his heart, to ensure that he will refuse Moses' entreaties:

> The LORD said to Moses, "When you return to Egypt, see that you perform before Pharaoh all the wonders I have given you the power to do. *But I will harden his heart so that he will not let the people go.* (Exodus 4:21–23)

And:

> You are to say everything I command you, and your brother Aaron is to tell Pharaoh to let the Israelites go out of his country. *But I will harden Pharaoh's heart,* and though I multiply my miraculous signs and wonders in Egypt, he will not listen to you. Then I will lay my hand on Egypt and with mighty acts of judgment I will bring out my divisions, my people the Israelites. (Exodus 7:2-5)

And again:

> Moses and Aaron performed all these wonders before
> Pharaoh, *but the LORD hardened Pharaoh's heart,* and he
> would not let the Israelites go out of his country. (Exodus
> 11:10)

For obvious reasons these passages have generated controversy
among theologians. God himself hardens the heart of Pharaoh
and then punishes the Egyptians for the results of his hardheart-
edness. How can this be fair?

Paul in his letter to the Romans was one of the first to address the issue, adopting a "shut up and stop asking questions"
strategy:

> For the Scripture says to Pharaoh: "I raised you up for this
> very purpose, that I might display my power in you and
> that my name might be proclaimed in all the earth." There-
> fore God has mercy on whom he wants to have mercy, and
> he hardens whom he wants to harden. One of you will say
> to me: "Then why does God still blame us? For who resists
> his will?" But who are you, O man, to talk back to God?
> "Shall what is formed say to him who formed it, 'Why did
> you make me like this?'" Does not the potter have the
> right to make out of the same lump of clay some pottery
> for noble purposes and some for common use? (Romans
> 9:17–21).

Others have tried to explain away the apparent injustice. They
argue that in fact *Pharaoh hardens his own heart.* As for the passages that indicate otherwise, they are either taken as metaphor-
ical or analyzed as a mistranslation based on the ambiguity of
the term "harden." Martin Luther reserves special contempt for
this kind of strategy:

So that, when God saith, "I will harden the heart of Pharaoh," you are to change the persons and understand it thus:—"Pharaoh hardens himself by My long-suffering" and dismiss it as a "liberty of interpretation, by a new and unheard-of kind of grammar," which only "goes to confound all things . . . . It is dangerous, nay, impious, thus to twist the Word of God, without necessity and without authority." (*The Bondage of the Will*, 195)

Luther goes on to employ a strategy similar to Paul's:

God is that Being, for whose will no cause or reason is to be assigned, as a rule or standard by which it acts; seeing that, nothing is superior or equal to it, but it is itself the rule of all things. . . . Wherefore, what God wills, is not therefore right, because He ought or ever was bound so to will; but on the contrary, what takes place is therefore right, because He so wills. A cause and reason are assigned for the will of the creature, but not for the will of the Creator; unless you set up, over Him, another Creator. (*The Bondage of the Will*, 215.)

Arguably, the most sophisticated response comes from Jonathan Edwards who uses this episode as part of his defense of Calvinistic compatibilism. Pharaoh's case shows that human beings can deserve blame even when God has determined their character and actions. His analysis bears a striking similarity to the classical compatibilism of Hume. Human beings are blameworthy when they perform an action that is motivated by a wicked or sinful desire. There is no need to go further to discover the cause of that sinful desire or sinful nature:

The Essence of the virtue and vice of dispositions of the heart, and acts of the will, lies not in their *cause*, but in their

nature. . . . Thus, for instance, ingratitude is hateful and
worthy of dispraise, according to common sense; not because something as bad, or worse than ingratitude, was the
Cause that produced it; but because it is hateful in itself, by
its own inherent deformity. (Edwards 1958 [1754], 59)

Edwards here explicitly rejects the incompatibilist TNR principle, the view that in order to be responsible for an action, you
have to be responsible, at least in part, for what causes the action. Edwards notes (again in the Humean manner) that when
it is supposed that nature, rather than God, implants evil dispositions in the hearts of men, "it is not commonly supposed that
men are worthy of no praise or dispraise for such dispositions
. . . ." And yet, "what is natural, is undoubtedly necessary" (Edwards 1958, 134). Since Pharaoh performed a wicked act that
stemmed from a wicked nature (his hardened heart), he is
blameworthy and deserves all the punishment God sends to
him. That God deliberately hardened his heart is irrelevant for
the purposes of assigning moral responsibility.

Of course, one man's *modus ponens* is another's *modus tollens*.
Manipulation cases like these have been used as counterexamples to classical compatibilism. What I wish to highlight about
Edwards' strategy, however, is not his conclusion, but rather the
way in which his theological commitments affect his view of the
conditions of responsibility. As a Calvinist theologian, he believes (1) that God fully determines human nature and behavior;
(2) that God blames and punishes human beings for their nature and behavior; and (3) that God cannot be unjust. For Edwards, these beliefs are non-negotiable, or at any rate less negotiable than his beliefs and intuitions about the conditions for
moral responsibility. It is certainly arguable that Edwards does
not find the TNR principle to be all that intuitive, since he so

confidently presents his position as one recommended by common sense. But even if Edwards were to feel, in his private moments, the tug of the incompatibilist intuition, it is clear that the strength of that intuition would pale in comparison to his religious convictions. The situation is clear. God hardens the hearts of Pharaoh and other sinners, and then punishes them for their sins. God is just. Therefore it is just to punish the hearts of sinners God has hardened. If human reason is offended it is because human reason is "blind, deaf, impious, and sacrilegious in all the words and works of God" and therefore dares to be "introduced as a judge of the words and works of God" (*Bondage of the Will*, 92).

The way in which Edwards arrived at his beliefs about the conditions for responsibility contrasts markedly with the way collectivist societies and honor cultures arrive at their beliefs. As I have argued above, beliefs about desert in such societies have their origin in intuitions that arise naturally out of the cultural environment. There is thus no problem or paradox of responsibility to resolve or explain away. By contrast, theologians such as Luther, Calvin, and Edwards are compelled to defend a view of responsibility that developed thousands of years before their time, and in a completely different environment. It is a view, moreover, that seems counterintuitive to their contemporaries. Their approach is to appeal to a conviction that is stronger than any intuition about the proper conditions for responsibility: the conviction that God is just.

Universalists will rightly pounce on this approach as evidence that variation in responsibility perspectives can be explained away. The disagreement between Luther and Erasmus, they may argue, is not over the conditions of moral responsibility. It is a debate about the literal truth of the scriptures. Luther's extreme form of compatibilism is grounded in his irrational religious beliefs. Erasmus, who was not fettered to the literal word of a document written thousands of years earlier, was better able to perceive the *truth* about moral responsibility and desert.

This universalist objection has force, I do not deny that. I would maintain, however, that the discussion of pharaoh's guilt is useful for my overall defense of metaskepticism. First, it is evidence of a radically different conception of justice that prevailed in the societies in which the story was conceived and developed. More importantly, Edwards' strategy illustrates an important point, one that I will develop at length in Part Two of this book: our intuitions about the conditions of responsibility, however strong, are always negotiable. We must examine how well they cohere with other intuitions, other beliefs that we hold to be true. When an inconsistency arises, there is no principled reason to *automatically* preserve our intuitions about responsibility and reject the beliefs that conflict with them. Many factors must be considered before making an all-things-considered final judgment. I do of course reject Luther's reasons for overriding his intuitions about the control condition for moral responsibility (assuming he had such intuitions, which is open to question). But his methodology seems to me perfectly sound. Luther preserved the beliefs about which he was most certain, the beliefs most central to his commitments—and this forced him to jettison a view of moral responsibility that requires control. We can all use this same methodology to change or revise our beliefs about the conditions of moral responsibility.[9] Lastly, I would remind universalists that Luther and Erasmus were products of similar cultural environments, and so it would not be surprising if they shared common starting intuitions about the conditions of moral responsibility. Thus, even if the disagreement between them can be comfortably explained away, this does not mean that disagreements between individuals living in very different cultural environments can be explained away in similar fashion.

Conclusion

At the end of the great Dashiell Hammett novel *The Maltese Falcon,* the femme fatale Brigid O'Shaughnessy asks Sam Spade how he could send her to prison. Spade answers with a long list of reasons to do so and then adds, "Maybe some of them of are unimportant. I won't argue about that. But look at the number of them. Now on the other side, we've got what?"

This is my question to the universalist: on the other side we've got what?

In chapters 2 and 3, I have appealed to evidence in a wide variety of disciplines to show that there are deep cross-cultural differences in perspectives about moral responsibility. I am aware that one can offer alternate explanations for any of the cases of variation I've described, explanations that do not involve essential differences in intuitions or attitudes about moral responsibility. No single study or piece of evidence can provide decisive proof for this part of the challenge. That is the nature of evidence-based arguments in general—decisive proofs are not possible. In every case, I have done my best to justify my view that the disagreements in question are disagreements about the conditions for appropriate assignments of moral responsibility. And the examples when *taken together* makes it plausible that there are deep intuitive differences across cultures about the conditions for moral responsibility and desert. As Sam Spade says, maybe some of the cases are unimportant. But look at the number of them. Now on the other side, we've got what?

In his discussion of collective responsibility, Heinrich Gomperz writes:

It is the Christian tradition that makes us feel today as if
group responsibility were but an archaic survival. But that
does not prove that collective, and still less social, responsibility is always and everywhere unreasonable . . . . Even
where its inapplicability has to be recognized, it is not because collective responsibility is necessarily impossible or
unreasonable, it is rather because, carried to an extreme, it
may run counter to the spirit of a given age. (1939, 336,
342)

It is human nature to believe that the principles of one's own
culture and time are objective, universally applicable truths. But
it is also a fallacy, and a dangerous one. It is not enough for the
universalist to point out that a favorable interpretation of the
data I have provided is *possible*. No interpretation can ever be
ruled out entirely. The universalist must show why it is *plausible*
that the evidence I have given does not support the existence of
cross-cultural differences concerning moral responsibility.

The universalist might also concede the existence of variation
about issues like collective responsibility and yet argue that
there is agreement on core intuitions concerning the narrower
concept of *individual* moral responsibility. My response to this
challenge is two-fold. First, research on the differences between
collectivist and individualist societies suggests that there is indeed variation relevant to the conditions for individual moral
responsibility. The Hamilton and Sanders studies, for example,
all focus on individuals who perform objectionable acts. Second, even if there were common ground on the issue of individual responsibility, this would still not vindicate most contemporary theories of responsibility. Both compatibilist and
incompatibilist theories are designed to determine the criteria
for fair assignments of blame and praise, period. It happens that

their criteria usually apply only to the individual who committed the act. Moral responsibility and individual moral responsibility match up almost perfectly on their accounts. But the ultimate aim of most theories of responsibility is to reveal the conditions under which everyone could be fairly blamed or praised.

Finally, many universalists may accept that there is genuine disagreement over conditions for responsibility, but deny that the differences undermine their theories. If cross-cultural and historical variation doesn't bother us in scientific inquiry, the universalist may ask, why should it bother us when it comes to moral responsibility? The question is a sensible one, and it is the task of chapter 4 to address it.

CHAPTER FOUR

Can the Variation Be Explained Away?

> The development of ideas of individual responsibility for
> crime is at root a response to problems of co-ordination and
> legitimation faced by systems of criminal law; the content
> and emphasis of these problems can be expected to change
> according to the environment in which the system operates.
> —Nicola Lacey, "In Search of the Responsible Subject"

THE UNIVERSALIST STRIKES BACK

In the last two chapters I have tried to demonstrate that there
are wide-ranging differences in perspectives about moral responsibility—in particular, variations in intuitions about the
conditions for fair or just assignments of blame, praise, punishment, and reward. In chapter 1, I raised objections to the views
of those philosophers who claim not to care about people's *intuitions* but instead to focus only on the *truth* about moral responsibility. Variation across cultures does not bother them; they
find it to be, at most, a matter of sociological interest. Yet these
same philosophers continue to appeal to intuitions in their
search for the "true" conditions of moral responsibility. But
there is a more sophisticated and less dismissive variant of this

objection one that is drawn from metaethical literature on disagreement. This response poses a serious threat to my thesis, and the bulk of this chapter will be devoted to assessing its plausibility.

The universalist may begin as follows: "I don't doubt that there is a great deal of variation in attitudes and beliefs about moral responsibility. I never expected otherwise. But the existence of this variation does not entail that there is no 'fact of the matter' about the true conditions for moral responsibility. After all, there is hardly an issue about which you will find universal agreement. People still disagree about our place in the solar system, yet no one argues for metaskepticism about astronomy. You may reply that scientific inquiry has produced consensus. But has it? Some 44 percent of students when polled do not believe *modus tollens* to be a valid form of inference. And as Sturgeon (2005) points out, there is nothing close to universal assent on the truth of evolutionary theory—the majority of Americans do not believe that we have evolved from the common ancestors of other species. What we mean, then, when we say that scientists have reached consensus is that there has come to be agreement among well-trained, competent inquirers. For a fair comparison, we should then presumably ask what the debate about moral responsibility has looked like when conducted by people who meet such minimum standards as being well and accurately informed about the relevant facts about human autonomy and having given careful thought to competing views and arguments. (Adapted from Sturgeon, 2005, 109)

"So [the universalist continues], we need not be too concerned about variations in attitudes and beliefs about these conditions. We should focus exclusively on the beliefs and attitudes of people who are reflective, open to dialogue, and accurately informed about relevant scientific and metaphysical facts—people, in other words, who are competent judges or inquirers.[1] In such a company we can expect a greater convergence of *considered judgments* about the conditions for moral responsibility. This analysis, moreover, fits within Heider's model of the five stages of responsibility attribution. (Heider 1958, 113) The collective responsibility one finds in honor cultures and in the doctrine of original guilt is at Heider's lowest stage. Honor killings and manipulation cases (such as the stories of Agamemnon and Pharaoh) belong to the second level, where 'anything caused by a person is ascribed to him.' In the third stage, the criteria are refined further so that individuals are only held responsible for offenses they could have foreseen (even if they did not intend them to occur). Moving up to the fourth level, one finds a control condition where agents are held responsible only for what they intend to do. And finally, when we advance to the fifth level, we examine factors that cause the agents to have the intention they have and recognize that the 'responsibility for the act is at least shared by the environment.' The crucial point is that we have made *progress* in our understanding of when it is fair to assign moral responsibility, advancing from the most primitive conception—blame and praise for acts that "are in any way connected with us"—to the most sophisticated, which requires that we explore the sources of our motives and intentions before assigning responsibility."

[The universalist then concludes:] "We see evidence of such progress even in the works of the Old Testament. In Deuteronomy the Lord claims that He will 'punish the faults of the sons and the grandsons and the great-grandsons of those who hate me.' But in the prophetic book of Ezekiel, understanding about the conditions for responsibility has already advanced. The Lord asks Ezekiel:

Why do you keep repeating this proverb in the land of
Israel—
*The fathers have eaten unripe grapes, and the children's
teeth are set on edge?*
... there will no longer be any reason to repeat this
proverb in Israel ... the man who has sinned, he is the one
who shall die. ... But you object, 'Why does the son not
suffer for the sins of his father?' The son, however, has
been law-abiding and honest, has kept all my ways and
followed them, and so he shall certainly live. The man
who has sinned is the one who must die; a son is not to
suffer for the sins of his father, nor a father for the sins of
his son. (Ezekiel 18)

The bottom line is this: In our search for the truth about moral
responsibility, we do not have to concern ourselves with primitive conceptions any more than the modern astronomer has to
worry about Ptolemaic or Aristotelian views of the solar system.
There is no reason to ignore the progress we have made to this
point. Rather, we must continue to advance our inquiry by developing arguments and theories that bring the intuitions of
competent judges about general principles and individual cases
into something like reflective equilibrium. This approach will
lead us to the truth about moral responsibility, just as it has
brought us closer to truth in other areas of inquiry, such as logic,
mathematics, and science."

A First Assessment of the Universalist Response

I believe that this type of universalist response is the most viable
strategy, perhaps the only viable strategy, for defending universalist theories of moral responsibility. As I have noted, it is anal-

ogous to the broader strategy of defending moral realism against arguments that appeal to the existence of widespread moral disagreement. Mackie (1977, 37) writes that his "argument from relativity has some force simply because actual variations in moral codes are more readily explained by the hypothesis that they reflect ways of life than by the hypothesis that they express perceptions, most of them seriously inadequate and badly distorted, of objective values."[2] Moral realists respond that much of this variation can be attributed to errors in reasoning, bias, superstition, and disagreement about non-moral matters. According to Sturgeon (2005), a large part of moral disagreement would disappear if everyone adopted the position of philosophical naturalism, as one could reasonably expect any competent moral judge to do. Smith (1994, 188–89) agrees, arguing that much seemingly entrenched moral disagreement is due to the fact that one party or the other "forms their moral belief in response to the directives of a religious authority rather than as a result of the exercise of their own free thought in concert with their fellows." And Boyd (1988, 123) writes that "careful examination will reveal . . . that agreement on non-moral issues would eliminate *almost all* disagreement about the sorts of moral issues which arise in ordinary moral practice." The universalist could take this same position as regards the varying views on moral responsibility that I described in chapters 2 and 3.

As Loeb (1998, 209) notes, however, "conjecture about what careful examination will reveal is no substitute for careful ex-.amination, and the latter is what is needed if we are to make further progress." Loeb's remark applies equally well to attempts to explain away disagreement over the conditions of moral responsibility. It is not enough to simply *assume* that disagreement is a result of errors in reasoning or ignorance about nonmoral facts (Doris and Stich 2005, Doris and Plakias 2007). One must furnish evidence to back the claim.

The science analogy that some moral realists develop is problematic for a number of reasons. First, in science there is much more agreement than there is in ethics about how to identify competent judges and grade expertise (McGrath 2008). Second, there is in science a near universally accepted method for resolving persistent disagreement—namely, the scientific method. Newtonian astronomy is considered an advance over Ptolemaic astronomy because Newton's theory has more predictive and explanatory power. When evaluating competing accounts of moral responsibility, there is no comparable methodology that might resolve the dispute. Consequently, in science, we have non-question-begging ways of identifying which parties are being irrational. Deciding that question is far more difficult when it comes to disagreement about moral issues, and even more so (I will argue) in the subset of moral questions that concern moral responsibility.

Two Challenges for the Universalist

The universalist response that I have outlined above relies on several controversial assumptions, including a crucial empirical assumption about the uniformity of human psychology; specifically, the assumption that once conceptual confusions are eliminated and non-moral facts agreed upon, human beings will achieve consensus on the criteria for justified assignments of moral responsibility—*no matter what their physical and social environment.* In what follows, I lay out two challenges to this assumption.

The Negative Challenge

The first challenge is a negative one. The goal here is to present well-developed examples of cultural perspectives on moral responsibility where the conditions of application differ radically from those favored by contemporary theories of responsibility, and then to challenge the universalist to explain precisely how the accounts are irrational or implausible. (See Doris and Plakias [2007] for an excellent elaboration of this strategy as it applies to ethical disagreement in general).

Consider the responsibility norms in the honor culture of Saga Iceland. They may seem arbitrary and unjust; and they are certainly, as Gomperz would put it, "contrary to the spirit of the age." They are elaborate and complex and have been the subject of endless discussion, analysis, and revision from within.[3] But in what sense are they irrational? Recall that when Hrafnkels took revenge on the brother of his torturer, a man who had nothing to do with the original offense, Sam (the brother) complained to the patrons. The patrons, who served as quasi-judges, supported Hrafnkels's decision and gave reasons for their endorsement. Theirs was a considered judgment that does not seem to have arisen from superstition or an incomplete knowledge of relevant non-moral facts. There do not seem to be grounds for thinking that more rational reflection would have caused the Icelanders to revise their intuitions or judgments about the conditions for responsibility. If there are such grounds, the universalist should point them out and not merely assume they exist.

The universalist might point out that the norms supporting Hrafnkels's judgments are no longer prevalent in contemporary Iceland. True, but is this an indication of the implausibility or irrationality of these norms? A look at the history of the changes in Iceland suggests not. Iceland was invaded and conquered by the British, who brought with them an entirely different set of norms. While the transformation in attitudes and values among the Icelandic people may be a result of "the exercise of their own free thought in concert with their fellows," it is more plausibly the result of a Christian culture imposing its values on a conquered people.

A more contemporary endorsement of a different perspective on moral responsibility can be found in Milan Kundera's *The Unbearable Lightness of Being*. Tomas, the hero of the novel, condemns his Czech countrymen for absolving themselves of responsibility for the evils of the communist regime on the grounds that they simply had no knowledge of the atrocities being committed:

> When Tomas heard Communists shouting in defense of their inner purity, he said to himself, "as a result of your 'not knowing,' this country has lost its freedom, lost it for centuries, perhaps, and you shout that you feel no guilt? How can you stand the sight of what you've done? How is it that you aren't horrified? Have you no eyes to see? If you had eyes, you would have to put them out and wander away from Thebes." (Kundera 1999, 177)

Here, Tomas is challenging the "epistemic condition" for responsibility: the view that in order to deserve blame for an act, one must have *known* that it was wrong, or must be culpable in some way for one's ignorance. Tomas (and Kundera too, almost certainly) finds it appalling that the Czechs would exonerate themselves simply because they did not know that it was wrong to support the communist regime. He regards an account of responsibility without epistemic condition not only rational but *morally superior*, at least in the circumstances the Czechs were facing. We might flinch at making the same endorsement, but there is no clear sense in which Tomas's (or Oedipus's) view of moral responsibility is irrational, primitive, or inferior.

The universalist will be quick to object that Tomas believes the Czechs are culpable for their ignorance about the evils of the

Soviet regime and that it is for this reason that he holds them responsible for their actions. Tomas blames them because they *should have known* about the atrocities committed in the name of communist ideals. But Tomas's use of the Oedipus analogy suggests otherwise. Oedipus could not have known that he was committing incest and patricide, but Tomas nonetheless applauds his decision to hold himself responsible for his deeds. But perhaps Tomas believes that Oedipus too was culpable for his ignorance . . . ? At this point, the metaskeptic may start to yank out his hair. Possibility is cheap; actuality is expensive.[4] It is the easiest thing in the world to suggest alternate explanations if you do not have to provide any positive support for them. Even if the metaskeptic begins with the burden of proof, there must be some way to eventually discharge it. If universalists can provide textual or empirical support for their alternate explanations, then they may advance the debate. But if the basis for their belief is nothing more than the conviction that these other perspectives on responsibility *must* be irrational, then they are simply begging the question.

One might also claim, as Nussbaum does in her classic article "Equity and Mercy," that Tomas's and Oedipus's way of regarding responsibility neglects crucial facts about an agent's *particularity*, his good character and fine intentions. According to Nussbaum, the rational way must take such agent particulars into account. The Greek notion of responsibility (*dikê*), Nussbaum writes, ignores "questions of motive and intention that one might think crucial in just sentencing" (1993, 90). But there is an important difference between neglecting particulars and being aware of them but not finding them relevant to the assignment of responsibility. Recall the discussion of differences between Japanese and American perspectives in which it was shown that the Japanese were equally aware of mental state considerations, but they did not find then as important as Americans did in determining an offender's responsibility. The same seems to be true of the Greeks. They do not *ignore* questions of motive and intention. They simply disagree with Nussbaum that such motives are crucial to just sentencing. To assume that an epistemic or control condition is essential for the just assignment of responsibility begs the question against the Greek perspective. Indeed, it seems that a Nussbaum counterpart in an honor culture or collectivist society could just as easily accuse Western cultures of neglecting crucial particulars in its own practices. When assigning responsibility in the U.S., we do not place much focus on the offender's social status, or on the familial associations of the offender and the offended party. We are not *neglecting* those particulars—we are often perfectly aware of them—but we do not find them relevant to determinations of an individual's blameworthiness. It is clear then that universalists need to do more than point out that a conception of responsibility neglects certain particulars; they must in addition show why it is more rational to take one set of particulars into account rather than another when determining an agent's responsibility.

As noted, the challenge in these examples is a negative one. I am not (yet) arguing that alternate conceptions of moral responsibility are as rational as those employed by philosophers working in the contemporary Western debate. Rather, my claim is that universalists have not yet identified the ways in which alternate conceptions are irrational. No matter what the field of inquiry, universalists face this burden when presented with widespread variation. The Darwinian, for example, can shoulder this burden by pointing to the religious convictions of many of critics of evolutionary theory and to their ignorance of the fossil record, morphology, and molecular biology. The defender of a universalist theory of responsibility can appeal to nothing of this kind. My goal, then, is to place the burden of proof on universalists who claim that disagreement among competing conceptions of responsibility can be explained away as a product of irrationality.

The weakness of the challenge is that it relies on certain (in my view plausible) assumptions about the burden of proof, an issue that generates even less agreement than moral responsibility. Michael McKenna (personal communication) writes:

> Not every challenge of burden of proof should be answered with a conciliatory effort to shoulder the burden. The racist comes to me and says that he rejects my claim that race has no bearing on the dignity of a person. He tells me to prove it. I can't see that it is my burden to do so, even if doing so is as easy as pie. The burden's on him to show why it is not.

The racist analogy is intriguing but problematic. First, the racist is making a positive claim that there is a reason to value one race more than another. He is placing an additional condition on human dignity and moral worth. Arguably, it is his burden to show why we should add this condition. By contrast, Oedipus and Tomas are denying that there should be an additional condition—the epistemic condition—on just assignments of moral responsibility. In a sense, then, it is those who place *additional* conditions on moral responsibility who are more closely analogous to the racist. Moreover, as I have argued, it is not obvious that theories of responsibility with an epistemic condition are morally superior. We may disagree with Tomas and Oedipus, or we may find their views counterintuitive, but it is not clear that we hold the moral high ground in this disagreement.

McKenna (personal communication) asks another reasonable question: "Why is it incumbent on others to offer the textual evidence [that variation can be explained away]? Why is the burden not on you?" And in fact I do agree that the burden is initially on the skeptic (or metaskeptic in this case). The evidence presented in chapters 2 and 3 constitutes my attempt to discharge that burden. But it is impossible to prove beyond a shadow of a doubt that one's interpretation of a text or piece of evidence is correct. There has to be some point at which the burden shifts from the metaskeptic to the universalist.

The Positive Challenge

The negative challenge aims to show that universalists have not adequately defended their position on the issue of moral responsibility. My next topic, the positive challenge, aims to provide positive reason to doubt the universalist assumption that disagreement in considered judgments about responsibility would dissolve under more ideal conditions of rationality. My strategy for developing this challenge is the following. First, I argue that the conditions we place on moral responsibility are examples of norms—norms that govern how much blame, praise, punishment, or reward should be assigned to norm violators. I then outline some leading accounts of the origins and underlying psychological architecture of norms. These accounts suggest that responsibility norms vary systematically with the ecology and social structure of the culture in which they emerge. I argue that if the variation in intuitions is deeply rooted in human psychological architecture, which in turn is influenced by social and physical environments, then it is unlikely that fully rational people would converge on the same considered judgments about the conditions of responsibility. So long as a there continues to be variation in human environments, consensus will not be achieved.

Sripada and Stich (2006) and Kelly and Stich (2007) characterize norms as follows: "A norm is a rule or principle that specifies actions which are required or forbidden within a group or culture." Norms are "intrinsically motivating"; that is, they motivate us to comply with them, independent of any instrumental reasons we might have to do so. (Or course, we are often instrumentally motivated to comply with them as well.) Relatedly, they have "independent normativity"—the rules are not essentially tied to an authority or dependent on any form of enforcement. They are passed on reliably within a group, and children acquire them early in life. There is a good deal of cultural conformity about the content of the rules *within* a particular culture, but substantial diversity about which behaviors are recommended or forbidden across cultures. Finally, violations of norms, when discovered, lead to punitive attitudes and sometimes to punishment as a means of enforcement.

With this list of features in mind, we can see that the conditions placed on responsibility do indeed qualify as norms. These conditions are rules that specify behavior, namely when it is appropriate to blame, praise, punish or reward someone. They are intrinsically motivating: we regard people as responsible for more than just instrumental reasons (indeed, this is the very nature of moral desert). They have independent normativity: someone can be morally responsible in the eyes of law, but not according to our criteria, and vice versa. The conditions of moral responsibility are supported by punishment. If someone in a group blames or punishes someone who does not meet the community's criteria for responsibility, they may be punished either by legal action (for "taking the law into their own hands") or by gossip and ostracism. This feature is even more evident in honor cultures, in which elders chastise and punish aggressive young men for unjustified retaliation (Miller 2006). Conversely, people who choose not to punish an offender who does meet the conditions of responsibility risk disgrace or accusations of engaging in "public violations of justice." Norms about the conditions of responsibility are universally present: there are no societies that do not place any conditions on just or fair assignments of blame and praise. They are passed on reliably, and individuals acquire them early in life. (My daughter had just turned three when she started claiming that her naughtier actions were "just an accident." And just recently, at six, she had her teddy bear Bebe say, "It's not my fault—my Daddy was a bad example!") There is a good deal of cultural conformity, agreement *within* a group about the criteria for moral responsibility. And finally, there is substantial *cross-cultural diversity* on the content of these conditions—as I have spent the last three chapters arguing. It appears, then, that conditions of moral responsibility can safely be regarded as norms—norms that govern how much blame, praise, punishment, or reward should be assigned to norm violators.

STEP TWO: THE ORIGINS OF NORMS

The next step in the challenge is to examine how responsibility norms originated. For this purpose, I turn to the Richerson and Boyd (2005) dual inheritance theory of human cooperation, in which norms play a starring role. As noted in chapter 2, Richerson and Boyd's models suggest that in order to secure cooperation in large groups, individuals must be willing to suffer minor costs incurred in punishing individuals who violate cooperative norms. With altruistic punishment in place, free-riders can be sufficiently deterred even in a large society and cooperative norms can flourish. According to Richerson and Boyd, the capacity to acquire, internalize, and comply with norms is innate, as is the disposition to punish norm violators. But the content of norms is not innate; it is passed on within the group via social transmission. This allows individuals to adapt to a changing environment much faster than if the traits were passed on genetically. An interesting wrinkle of Richerson and Boyd's theory is that altruistic punishment and biased transmission can stabilize a wide variety of norms within a culture or group—including norms that are maladaptive. This process can lead, Richerson and Boyd argue, to cultural group selection. For example, suppose Group A and Group B are competing for resources and there is a change in their environment. Group A is in the grip of norms that are not well suited to the new environment, while Group B's norms allow them to adapt to the change. Group B can now out-compete Group A, and Group B's norm variants will spread widely through the population. The losing group (Group A) does not have to be wiped out; they may simply assimilate into the victorious group while retaining at least some of their own cultural variants. Even if there is no direct competition between groups, a "prestige bias" may cause people to imitate the norms of their more successful neighbors, causing the most effective norms to spread within their own population.

This model has two important implications. First, the existence of norms and the punishment of violations are human universals. In order to adapt quickly to their environment, human beings must have the capacity to acquire norms from their social environment and to behave in accordance with those norms. Second, we should expect a great deal of variation in the *content* of these norms. Environments across the world pose a wide variety of challenges to survival and prosperity. Different norms are better suited to different environments. And since the process of norm transmission generates changes in a culture's social environment, there is a snowball effect whereby new norms develop as responses to these changes.

STEP THREE: THE PSYCHOLOGICAL ARCHITECTURE OF NORMS

Sripada and Stich (2006) offer a model describing the psychological mechanisms that underlie the process of norm acquisition and implementation. The function of the acquisition mechanism, according to the authors, is "to identify behavioral cues indicating that a norm prevails in the local cultural environment, to infer the content of that norm, and to pass information about the content of the norm on to the implementation system, where it is stored and used." (2006, 291) The acquisition mechanism begins to operate early in life as children observe and internalize the norms of their group. It is automatic, not something they can choose to turn on or off. The implementation mechanism then stores the norms and motivates norm compliance and punitive behavior towards norm violators. Emotions like moral outrage or resentment play a pivotal role in the implementation mechanism, providing the intrinsic motivation to punish violators. Sripada and Stich's model complements the Richerson and Boyd theory which posits as a universal phenomenon the willingness to punish norm violators at a cost. Other attitudes, such as guilt and shame, may also motivate norm compliance. Finally, according to Sripada and Stich's model, these norms and emotions interact to generate moral intuitions and judgments. Sometimes the norms and emotions determine the judgments, which, if they are rationally justified at all, are justified by post-hoc reasoning (Haidt 2001). The model allows as well for moral reasoning to play a causal role in the formation of moral and beliefs judgments, although rarely will moral reasoning be the whole story.[5]

We can now apply these models to the specific norms governing the conditions of moral responsibility. As I argued in chapter 2, the functions of responsibility norms differ according on the environment of the group. In honor culture environments, it is important to project the image of the hair-trigger retaliator. The normative focus is therefore on offended parties, and considerations regarding the motives for the offense are de-emphasized. In more institutionalized environments, by contrast, the primary function of retribution is not to reinforce the reputation of the group or the individual, but rather to discourage free-riding behavior in general. State of mind factors are quite relevant to the question of whether the offender will commit future offenses, and so we would expect them to play a much larger role in judgments of blameworthiness and desert. Norms specifying conditions of responsibility that are compatible with these functions can emerge within a group over short time periods, grounded in physiological processes that motivate specific emotional responses to wrongdoing. These emotions and norms give rise to differences in core intuitions and beliefs—the starting points for reflective equilibrium—about when it is fair to blame, praise, punish, and reward ourselves and others.

The differences between collectivist and individualist attitudes about responsibility are similarly rooted in the social structures and environments of their respective cultures. In chapter 3, I described several impressively large studies that document significant variation in the importance of such factors as the mental state of the offender, role relationships, and external influence. I showed how cultural psychologists regard these attitudes as arising out of distinct conceptions of the self, which are products of the cultural and physical environment in which they appear.

THE CHALLENGE CONCLUDED

We can now bring together all the threads we have been following to illuminate the positive challenge posed to the universalist. Environments across the world pose a wide variety of challenges to groups trying to survive and prosper. Different norms are better suited for different environments. Norms relating to moral responsibility and the conditions of its application:

1. vary dramatically across cultures;
2. are often adapted to the particular environment in which they appear, transmitted by social learning processes;
3. are internalized early in life, becoming deeply rooted in our psychologies; and
4. give rise to strong emotional and physiological responses, which in turn . . .
5. . . . form the basis for our core intuitions concerning both particular cases and the general principles for assigning blameworthiness and praiseworthiness.</nlt>

Thus, the models of Richerson and Boyd and Stich and Sripada suggest that the variation in intuitions about responsibility is deeply entrenched in our cognitive architecture. And these intuitions, as I demonstrated in chapter 1, ultimately ground our theories of moral responsibility. How then can the universalist plausibly suppose that fully rational people would converge in their considered judgments about the conditions of moral responsibility?

I am in no way claiming that once these norms are in place, critical reflection cannot affect our considered intuitions and judgments. As I have noted above, reason can play a role in the modification of norms. Sorting out errors of reasoning and learning relevant non-moral facts will almost certainly lead to significant advances in our understanding of moral responsibility. Philosophical analysis may cause us to revise our considered judgments about responsibility—and these changes could very well be substantial within a particular culture. However, given that the disagreement in intuitions and attitudes is not, at bottom, a product of errors of reasoning or ignorance of non-moral facts, it is implausible that reflection and dialogue would cause different cultures to arrive at the *same* considered judgments about the conditions of moral responsibility. Nor is there any reason why they should. If norms that support a view of responsibility with a de-emphasized control condition are well adapted to a particular environment, then it is unclear how we could justly accuse individuals who observe those norms of being irrational *in those environments*. It may be that the conditions for true blameworthiness that arise from intuitions formed in Western environments simply have no place in other kinds of environments. And since appeals to intuitions ultimately ground our theories of responsibility, there is nothing to ground the applicability of individualistic conditions in environments for which they are ill suited.

Objections and Replies

It is possible that one might accept the bulk of the above analysis, but claim that it nevertheless does not support a position as radical as metaskepticism about responsibility. One might argue that it supports, instead, only the much more moderate view that under certain conditions societies cannot afford to operate according to true principles of moral responsibility. When there is scarcity of resources and no dependable form of law enforcement, perhaps there is no alternative but to abandon the control condition and punish relatives of offenders. The practice is still fundamentally unfair, but it is a necessary evil or at most "second best" morally speaking, and can only be justified in such unfavorable conditions.[6] Indeed, the legal doctrine of "strict liability," according to which individuals or corporations can be held responsible regardless of fault, is an example of such an attitude. The doctrine is motivated entirely by utilitarian considerations and is restricted to a very small range of areas, most notably to product liability and to extremely hazardous industries. In those contexts it is regarded as unfair but necessary for practical reasons under certain circumstances. Perhaps the attitudes in honor cultures and the practice of collective responsibility can be regarded in a similar fashion.

This objection is a serious threat to my position, because it affirms the existence of real universally applicable conditions for moral responsibility. The argument would run as follows: True blameworthiness for an action requires that the individual perform the action (or be culpable in some way for its being performed), and that he do so with a significant degree of control. Under some circumstances and in some environments, however, this (accurate) understanding of moral responsibility is simply not viable. An unfair and inaccurate set of rules about responsibility must be put in place for practical reasons. If this argument is sound, my metaskeptical thesis is false, although it might still offer some practical insights about the viability of true systems of responsibility.

Fortunately for metaskepticism, I do not think the argument sound. For one thing, it underestimates the moral benefits of collectivist attitudes about responsibility. As Feinberg in his classic paper on the topic remarks, collective responsibility not only expresses the solidarity of the group but strengthens it as well (1968, 677). Collective responsibility therefore promotes a moral good to the extent that group solidarity is a moral good. Furthermore, feelings of collective responsibility are bound up with feelings of sympathetic identification. Consider the feelings of responsibility we feel for the acts of our children. We take pride in their accomplishments and feel shame and responsibility for any wrongdoing on their part. A cynic might claim that we are only feeling pride or shame for our own role in raising them, but as most people who have children know, this is simply not the case. As Feinberg notes, the responsibility we feel for our children is genuinely vicarious—it is an expression and a reinforcement of love and solidarity. In my view, this is a real moral good, not one that is morally "second best" but necessary for practical reasons.

Feinberg goes on to discuss the "frankpledge" system of collective responsibility that existed in England between the eleventh and fifteenth centuries. Under the terms of Anglo Saxon law, groups of approximately ten people, connected by kinship or friendship, were jointly responsible for the criminal acts of each of its members. Feinberg considers the view that such a system is the "barbarous expedient of a people who had no conception of individualistic justice," but he finds that judgment too severe. He writes:

> The frankpledge system was a genuine system of criminal law. There was nothing arbitrary, *post-hoc*, or *ex post facto* about it. It was also a system of compulsory group self-policing in an age when professional policing was impossible. Moreover, it reinforced a pre-existing group solidarity the like of which cannot occur in an age of rapid movement like our own. Most importantly, the system worked; it pre-

vented violence and became *generally accepted as part of
the expected natural order of things.* (Feinberg 1968, 680,
my italics)

Feinberg seems to reject the idea that a collectivist understanding of moral responsibility is obviously false and morally inferior. On the other hand, he also objects to Gomperz's claim that a wholesale rejection of collective responsibility "mistakes a principal characteristic of individualistic ages for an eternal law of human nature" (see chapter 3, lead quote). Gomperz's claim, Feinberg writes, "misleadingly suggests a kind of historical relativism according to which individualistic and collectivist ages alternate like fashions in ladies skirts" (1968, 680). According to Feinberg, something like the frankpledge system could never function in our modern age of anonymous interactions and professional policing. The changes in modern times, Feinberg claims, have come about quite inevitably and are here to stay, "unless massive destruction forces the human race to start all over again" (680).

I would note two things about Feinberg's objection to Gomperz. First, Feinberg seems to be making a descriptive claim here rather than a moral one. In his view, the social and political structure of our current environment is one in which individualistic perspectives are suitable—and nothing in the remotely foreseeable future will change this. He is *not* claiming that this is morally the best state of affairs; indeed, he goes on to list some moral and practical costs that the individualistic perspective entails. He agrees with Gomperz that the principle of individual responsibility is not an eternal law. Second, as I have tried to demonstrate in the previous chapters, Feinberg's descriptive claim is inaccurate, obviously so if he means it to apply to the entire world rather than just to the United States. There are many present-day cultures whose environments more closely resemble that of twelfth-century England than twenty-first-century urban America. If anything, *we* in the United States are the outliers, the weird ones (Henrich et al. 2011). So it may be that neither set of norms and attitudes is morally "second-best." They both have moral advantages and disadvantages, and each is only appropriate in certain environments. When functioning properly, these two conceptions of moral responsibility can be 'tied for first," morally speaking.

Universalists may still protest that holding people responsible only for what is in their control is clearly, *self-evidently*, more fair and therefore morally superior to any alternative conception. But here, as elsewhere, I would claim that the universalist is making an unwarranted generalization based on his or her own intuitions. Unless universalists provide evidence that their conception of fairness would be shared by reflective individuals in other cultures, there is no reason to take their claims about self-evidence seriously. It may help to view this issue from another perspective as well. As I discussed in chapter 3, the differences between collectivist and individualistic perspectives are differences of degree and not kind. We should think of them as points on a continuum with Americans on the far end of the individualist side. But there is further for Americans to go. We might, for example, become what the cynic imagines us to be: people who no longer take pride in the achievements of our children except to the extent that we ourselves have played a conscious role in bringing about those achievements. We might no longer feel responsible for and ashamed of the wrongdoing of our children and siblings except when we consciously contributed in some way to its occurrence. And we might eventually find this view of responsibility self-evident. After all, how could it be fair to blame or praise parents for actions that they

did not play a role in bringing about and could not have prevented from occurring? Perhaps this move towards an even
more radical form individualism will occur. But would that be
something to celebrate? Is it self-evident that this would constitute moral progress? I have my doubts on all these counts. We
might do well to be wary of asserting too confidently that views
situated at the collectivist end of the spectrum are less rational
and morally inferior to our own.[7]

The final objection I will consider here is one that takes an indirect approach to demonstrating the irrationality of competing
conceptions of responsibility. One might argue that we should
reject the attitudes of Bedouins or Corsicans, say, because of the
immorality of other practices in which they engage that are not
directly related to moral responsibility. In chapter 2, for example, I discussed the practice of honor killings as evidence that
some honor cultures are not greatly concerned with intention
when assigning blame. Assuming I find honor killings immoral
(and I do),[8] doesn't this suggest that the culture's failure to take
the intention of the victim into account is also irrational and
immoral?

I think the answer is no, because the immorality of the practice has nothing to do with moral responsibility. We condemn
honor killings because the practice of killing women for having
extramarital sex (whether it was intended or not) is morally abhorrent. Whether one ought to take intention into account
when assigning responsibility and whether one ought to endorse honor killings are separate questions. We do not dismiss
the founding fathers' conception of individual justice and responsibility because they endorsed the practice of slavery. If we
accepted only the intuitions of cultures with unimpeachable
moral practices across the board, there would be no intuitions
to accept. In addition, much of the variation I have described

comes from societies that we have no reason to think are any less *broadly* moral than our own. The bottom line is that we must evaluate attitudes about responsibility on their own merits. If we want to call them irrational, we must do more than show that the culture in which they are present has irrational or immoral beliefs about matters that are unrelated to moral responsibility.

CONCLUSION

This completes my case for the metaskeptical thesis, the view that there are no universally true conditions for moral responsibility. The evidence suggests that there would be no convergence in considered intuitions, even in idealized conditions of rationality. Since considered intuitions ultimately ground our theories of responsibility, there does not seem to be a principled way of establishing conditions of moral responsibility that would apply across cultures. Like all empirically driven arguments, this one could turn out be wrong. But my case is sufficiently strong, I believe, to shift the burden of proof to those who defend universalist theories. They must defend the empirical and theoretical assumptions on which their theories rely— or give a convincing account of why such a defense is unnecessary. In Part Two of this book, I will assume the truth of my thesis and go on to examine the implications of a metaskeptical view of the conditions of moral responsibility.

PART II

The Implications of Metaskepticism

CHAPTER FIVE

Where Do We Go from Here?

Part One of this book argued for metaskepticism about moral responsibility. The remainder of the book will be devoted to examining the implications of this position. My goal in this chapter is to identify where metaskepticism fits within the philosophical landscape and to outline a framework for how we might proceed if the theory is true. First I will explore the similarities and differences between metaskepticism and other nontraditional and skeptical positions about moral responsibility, focusing especially on the fascinating work of Richard Double. Next, I will consider some social and political implications of metaskepticism. Finally, I will lay out a framework for approaching issues of moral responsibility while remaining consistent with the broader metaskeptical thesis.

METASKEPTICISM AND OTHER NON-TRADITIONAL VIEWS ABOUT MORAL RESPONSIBILITY

Metaskepticism and "First-Order" Skepticism

One might wonder why metaskepticism doesn't collapse into straightforward skepticism or hard incompatibilism (as Pereboom terms the position) about moral responsibility. After all, if metaskepticism is true, there is no objectively true set of sufficient conditions that agents must meet in order to be responsible for their behavior. Matters are not so simple, however, because metaskepticism denies that there are universally true *necessary* conditions for moral responsibility as well. A first-order skeptic or denier of moral responsibility, like Strawson or Pereboom, holds that everyone is *not* morally responsible because everyone fails to meet a universally true necessary condition for the application of moral responsibility.[1] The metaskeptic, by contrast, holds that for any agent x, it's not the case that x is morally responsible (objectively, universally) and it is not the case that x is not morally responsible. There is no objective fact of the matter about whether the agent is morally responsible. The first-order responsibility skeptic believes that it is never fair to hold people morally responsible for their behavior, no matter what society they live in. The metaskeptic believes that is neither objectively fair nor objectively unfair.

One might argue that if metaskepticism is true, then the concept "moral responsibility" is empty—it does not refer to anything. Therefore the claim "x is not morally responsible" must be true. Consider the concept "unicorn"; it is empty, so the claim "x is not a unicorn" is always true.[2] But this analogy only holds if we assume that "moral responsibility," like "unicorn," is essentially a non-relative concept. Unicorns either exist or they don't, there is no middle ground. But moral responsibility is not such a clear-cut concept. Consider another analogy: the concept "good Oliver Stone movies." From my perspective, the concept is empty. (I do not count *Scarface* which Stone wrote but did not direct.) At the same time, the claim "*Born on the Fourth of July* is a good Oliver Stone movie" is not objectively false. From some perspectives, bizarre though they appear to me, the claim might well be true. Similarly, it may be that from some perspectives, moral responsibility has conditions that cannot be met, whereas from others, the conditions for moral responsibility are easily met. As long as this state of affairs is conceptually possible, metaskepticism is a substantively different position from other first-order skeptical views.[3]

Metaskepticism and Variantism

Knobe and Doris (forthcoming), and Doris, Knobe and Woolfolk (2007) have assembled an impressive array of evidence to support a position they call "variantism about moral responsibility." They claim (correctly) that virtually all existing theories of moral responsibility are invariantist—meaning that they employ the common assumption that "people should apply the *same* criteria in *all* of their moral responsibility judgments" (Knobe and Doris, forthcoming). Evidence from psychology, however, suggests that people vary their criteria for responsibility according to the context of the act. They apply different criteria for the acts of friends and the acts of strangers, good acts and bad acts, acts that cause severe harm and acts that cause mild harm, and so on. The primary difference between metaskepticism and variantism is that the latter focuses on *intrapersonal* differences of intuitions about responsibility, whereas my focus is on interpersonal variation. Consequently, the opponent of the metaskeptic is the universalist and not the invariantist. A theory may be invariantist but not universalist if it employs the same criteria for responsibility judgments across contexts but restricts the criteria's application to a specific culture. For example, one might propose an invariantist necessary condition for responsibility—say, reason-responsiveness—but claim that the condition only applies in certain cultures (Western cultures or "reason cultures" perhaps). Conversely, a theory can be variantist but universalist if the ways in which the criteria vary with context is meant to apply across cultures. Thus, a variantist theory might lay out condition x for the blameworthiness of family members and condition y for the blameworthiness of strangers. If the theory is universalist, condition x applies in all cultures when the agent is a family member, and condition y applies in all cultures when the agent is a stranger. Indeed, I believe that Knobe and Doris lean towards a universalist version of variantism.

My tentative view is that variantist theories, universalist or not, are unsatisfying because of what Knobe and Doris, following Vargas (2004), term "normative adequacy" considerations. If our goal is to develop a comprehensive view of when blame and praise are justified, varying our criteria according to factors like relatedness seems unacceptably arbitrary. It is more tempting to revise our intuitions when there is a conflict and retain the invariantist conditions. Of course, one might make the same point against the metaskeptic: the idea that a certain set of conditions for moral responsibility apply in some cultures but not others also seems unacceptably arbitrary—so metaskepticism fails normative adequacy requirements as well. But there is an important difference between the two cases. We are capable of revising our intuitions and considered judgments about responsibility in order to make them consistent (and invariantist). It is much more difficult to revise the intuitions and considered judgments of people in other cultures.

Metaskepticism and Dualism

Like the variantist position, Smilansky's (2000) dualist position rejects the notion that we must be either compatibilist or incompatibilist in all of our moral responsibility judgments. He argues that there are elements of truth in both positions that must be recognized. There is a basic sense in which it is *unfair* to punish people who are not the ultimate source of their actions. But there are also morally legitimate distinctions that only compatibilism can capture. For example, in the ultimate sense, it is unjust to punish and blame a thief who consciously chooses to steal, and endorses that choice. But according to Smilansky, there is a real sense in which it is *more* unjust to blame or punish a kleptomaniac. The hard determinist, Smilansky claims, finds the cases morally equal when in fact they are not.

It is not clear to me how Smilansky is justified in drawing a responsibility-grounding distinction between the kleptomaniac and the common thief. But I do not intend to mount a critique of dualism here. (I will return to the issue of dualism in chapter 6.) Rather, I wish to point out a crucial difference between dualism and metaskepticism: namely, that dualism is universalist to its core. According to Smilansky, incompatibilist and compatibilist perspectives "capture part of the ethical truth on free will, being equally derived from the basic free-will related ethical intuition—the Core Conception requiring concern with control for respect for persons" (Smilansky 2000, 100). Dualism thus means to capture truths about the conditions for moral responsibility, truths that apply across cultures. If my arguments about the variation of "free-will related ethical intuitions" are successful, they would undermine dualism no less than any other universalist theory of moral responsibility.

Metaskepticism and Revisionism

Vargas (2004, 2007) has recently developed a revisionist position on free will and moral responsibility. He agrees with skeptics like Strawson and Pereboom that our current conception of moral responsibility is incompatibilist, tied to ideas about ultimate origination as a requirement for blameworthiness and praise-worthiness. He argues, however, that rather than eliminating these concepts as the skeptics would, we ought to revise our views about the conditions for responsibility to make them compatible with a scientific understanding of human behavior. These revised conditions, according to Vargas, should resemble those of the compatibilist and involve sensitivity on the part of agents to moral reasons. Thus, Vargas's descriptive account of common-sense beliefs about moral responsibility is incompatibilist, but his prescriptive theory of responsibility—of how we *should* regard the conditions for responsibility—is compatibilist. Due in large part to philosophy of language considerations, Vargas does not find it especially problematic that his descriptive and prescriptive theories differ on some key points. According to externalist theories of reference, the properties associated with a concept at a certain time do not necessarily fix the reference of that concept. The concepts of whales, water, and race, for example, have properties we did not associate with them at one time, thanks to advances in empirical understanding. But these advances did not cause us to become eliminativists about these concepts. Instead, we revised the concepts to bring them in line with the knowledge we acquired. According to Vargas, we should do the same with the concept of moral responsibility.

If Vargas means his revisionism to apply across cultures, then the arguments I advanced in Part One have the potential to undermine both the descriptive and the prescriptive elements of his account. An analysis of collectivist societies and honor cultures, for example, raises doubts about the claim that the commonsense view of responsibility is universally incompatibilist. Indeed, the depth of the variation in these intuitions suggests that there *is* no single commonsense concept of moral responsibility across cultures. Similarly, the different features of the social and physical environments that individuals in these cultures face make it unlikely that there is a single concept of responsibility that *ought* to be embraced universally. Vargas's prescriptive compatibilist theory with its reason-responsiveness condition might serve the needs of a relatively individualistic culture like America while at the same time providing too restrictive, or too permissive, a condition for cultures that face different social and ecological challenges.

Metaskepticism and Honderich's "Attitudinism"

Like the dualist, Ted Honderich (1988) argues that neither compatibilism nor incompatibilism is true. But whereas Smilansky tries to develop *a priori* ethical claims to justify his view, Honderich focuses on the different attitudes people have that support both incompatibilist and compatibilist theories. Knowing that we cannot rise above the influences of our heredity and environment, according to Honderich, generates feelings of dismay—in this, he agrees with the incompatibilist, especially the libertarian. At the same time, Honderich argues that we have another set of "life-hopes" that require only that our actions be voluntary in the compatibilist sense. There are, moreover, some advantages to dwelling on the determined nature of our actions. Doing so can produce feelings of what he calls "satisfied intransigence—"everything is OK, nothing changes" (Honderich 1993, 86). Honderich does not, therefore, agree with compatibilists that the truth of determinism has no consequences at all for free will and responsibility. There are consequences, but they are different from those the incompatibilist imagines.

Richard Double (1996) makes two important points about Honderich's view. First, he notes that it might best be classified as a kind of incompatibilism. Like both libertarians and skeptics, Honderich argues that determinism rules out retributive attitudes and deserved punishment. And though Honderich suggests otherwise, incompatibilists do not deny that voluntariness of a certain kind is compatible with determinism, nor do they deny that this type of freedom is desirable. Honderich replies that incompatibilists give "no importance to the idea of freedom as just voluntariness" and that "following Kant, they supposed it to be something like the contrivance of philosophers." (1996, 858) But while Kant and some like-minded libertarians may share this dismissive attitude, skeptics like Strawson and Pereboom (as well as Sommers [2007a]) certainly do not. Even contemporary libertarians like Kane are not nearly as dismissive of voluntariness as Honderich claims. Double is right, then, that Honderich's view resembles that of a reasonable incompatibilist.

Double's second criticism is quite interesting and important for the purposes of my thesis. He faults Honderich for concluding that determinism has objective consequences of any kind. Double writes:

> If our responses to determinism are simply attitudes, and if attitudes are neither true nor false, then determinism has no logical, moral, or psychological consequences in the sense of *correct conclusions* that have to be accepted by all rational persons. There are only reactions to determinism, none of which is objectively better than all the rest. (Double 1996, 848)

Here Double argues that the non-cognitivist nature of Honderich's position dooms his "objective synthesis" of the two leading positions of freedom and responsibility from the start. Attitudes have no truth values, so there can be no objectively reasonable position to adopt. To drive home the point, Double imagines a "smart aleck" who denies that incompatibilist intuitions and attitudes count as evidence for incompatibilist conclusions about responsibility. He demands a *reason* for thinking that they do. And attitudes, the smart aleck claims, are not reasons.

Honderich has an available reply. Double's mistake, he writes, is that he ignores:

> ... that we *do* in fact share standard factual reasons having to do with voluntariness and origination for desires, evaluation, and entailment. We do have these factual reasons, settled ones, which enter into and support moral disapproval as certainly as we base our hopes in such factual propositions about our future actions, or a feeling of gratitude in such propositions about another's action, or confidence in our beliefs in such propositions about activities of inquiry. I have the human nature I have, not the nature of a Martian or a lunatic, despite the little truths about facts not entailing values and an attitude as a whole not having a truth value. (Honderich 1996, 859–60)

Honderich here points out that determinism does entail certain facts we all can recognize. And since human nature dictates that we have certain attitudes towards those facts, this gives us a reason for embracing a particular view about the consequences of determinism. I believe Honderich is right that Double's standards for what would count as a reason for embracing a particular view are too high. At the same time, Honderich's reply, and the prospects for his objective synthesis, rest on a key assumption, namely that all normal humans—as opposed to lunatics and Martians—share (or would share) his attitudes about the consequences of determinism. The evidence from Part One of this book casts serious doubt on the plausibility of this assumption. To take just one example, it seems that members of East Asian collectivist societies would not react with "dismay" at the prospect of not being able to rise above the influences of heredity and environment. The ambition to "rise above" is intimately connected to the individualistic quest for autonomy and a self distinct from that of others. As discussed in chapter 3, collectivist societies frown upon members of a group who wish to rise above the influence of their group, never mind the combined influences of the group, heredity, and other aspects of their environment. They do not attempt to separate themselves from these influences to the same extent as people do in the individualistic West. Plausibly, then, the knowledge that we cannot rise above these influences would not cause much dismay at all.

It would seem then that you do not have to be a smart aleck to question the incompatibilist aspect of Honderich's objective synthesis. You simply have to be one of presumably millions (billions perhaps) of people with attitudes about the determinist thesis that differ from Honderich's. Ultimately, then, I agree with Double that there are no consequences of determinism that *all* rational persons are compelled to accept. And this is one of the primary differences between my position and Honderich's.

Metaskepticism and Free Will Subjectivism

The previous discussion leads me to the final position I will consider: the position that Double termed "metacompatibilism" and later "free will subjectivism." According to Double, compatibilist and incompatibilist theories amount to nothing more than subjective attitudes about free will, moral responsibility, and their connection with determinism. Consequently, there is no fact of the matter about whether compatibilism or incompatibilism is correct.

The argument for metacompatibilism is as follows.[4]

1. If there is an answer to the dispute between compatibilists and incompatibilists, then moral responsibility is an objective property that a person might instantiate in certain situations.
2. Moral responsibility, if it is exists, is a moral property.
3. If there is an answer to the dispute over the correct analysis of moral responsibility, then at least one class of moral properties are objective properties that might be instantiated under certain conditions.
4. There can be no objective moral properties.
5. So, there is no answer to the dispute between compatibilists and incompatibilists over the correct analysis of moral responsibility.

The free will subjectivist and the metaskeptic share roughly the same conclusion, stated in premise (5). Although Double is sometimes lumped in with first-order skeptics on the issue of free will, it is clear that his argument, if successful, would also undermine the hard incompatibilism of Derk Pereboom and Galen Strawson. To see where the metaskeptic and the free will subjectivist differ, it is helpful to go through Double's argument. Metaskeptics accept the first three premises, with the caveat that it must at least be possible that objective moral properties are naturalistic properties. The question then is, what kind of objective moral property would moral responsibility have to be? Double does not commit himself to an answer, but I follow Wallace (1994) in defining the property of moral responsibility in terms of the fairness or appropriateness of holding someone morally responsible.

Premise (4) is where my argument veers away from Double's. Double's argument against metaethical objectivism is a clear and distilled version of familiar arguments put forward by Mackie (1977) and Harman (1977). Consequently, it is vulnerable to critiques from what Doris and Plakias (2008) call "convergentist" moral realists who argue that moral properties can be identified in terms of attitudes, beliefs, or judgments that people would converge upon under ideal conditions of rationality.[5] Unlike Double and Mackie, I see the convergentist strategy as a plausible analysis of what *could* constitute objective moral facts, including facts about moral responsibility. If there were a set of actions that would be universally condemned by fully rational people, then I think it would make sense to call those actions objectively wrong (or to assign the property of universal wrongness to the act). And if there were universal agreement about the conditions under which we should hold agents blameworthy for committing wrong actions, then it would make sense to call the agents objectively blameworthy for committing them.

To undermine such theories, one would have to show either that this analysis of moral properties is faulty or that there is no single conclusion about the conditions of moral responsibility that people would reach under ideal conditions of rationality. Double's argument commits him to the former strategy, while mine commits me to the latter. Double's has the advantage of not requiring the empirical support I have tried to provide. But that is the weakness of his argument as well. It requires that one rule out *a priori* the possibility of a naturalistic ethical realism, and, arguably, it places implausibly high standards on what would count as an objective moral property. My position accepts the possibility of naturalistic universalist theories of responsibility, but argues that such theories are empirically implausible given the nature of variation in attitudes and intuitions.

Thus, Double and I take very different routes to reach our conclusions. According to Double, our responses to determinism boil down to attitudes. Since attitudes are subjective expressions and do not have truth-makers, compatibilist and incompatibilist claims have no truth-makers either. I accept that claims about the conditions of responsibility may have truth-makers, those that involve the considered judgments of rational people upon reflection. However, the evidence put forward in Part One indicates that such a convergence of judgments about the conditions of responsibility is not possible, and, consequently, that there is no fact of the matter about whether someone is objectively blameworthy or praiseworthy for their behavior.

Another difference between my view and Double's concerns the "Where do we go from here?" question. According to Double, free will subjectivists "commit no logical error when they decide to hold strong views about moral responsibility despite their belief in free will subjectivism or to hold mild views because they believe their views are only subjective" (2003, 520). Double's broader metaethical subjectivism commits him to this view—there is no fact of the matter about how one should *respond* to the truth of free will subjectivism. We can believe that moral responsibility has any conditions we wish, and we can believe this as strongly or as weakly as we wish. We can either be "sheepish subjectivists" and hold tempered views about when people are blameworthy or praiseworthy, or we can be "strident subjectivists" and hold our views about moral responsibility as strongly as any realist. Double calls P. F. Strawson a strident subjectivist compatibilist and Bruce Waller a strident subjectivist hard determinist. (Double himself claims to waffle between these two positions.) Essentially, Double argues that we choose any means of responding to subjectivism about moral responsibility, depending on our whims and preferences.

CHAPTER FIVE

I believe Double moves too quickly to this "anything goes" conclusion. Our disagreement on this point stems from my tentative acceptance, and his denial, of the existence of truth-makers for claims about the conditions of moral responsibility. Because I believe that claims about moral responsibility *could* be true, I find more room to distinguish between reasonable and unreasonable responses to the truth of metaskepticism. Indeed, like many universalists, I advocate using something very much like wide reflective equilibrium for determining the most reasonable view. The only difference between myself and the universalist is that my goal is to determine what conditions of responsibility are reasonable *for me* to accept, while the universalist wishes to determine what is reasonable for everyone to accept. If my all-things-considered judgments coincide with those of other people, we will have arrived at a shared view about the conditions of responsibility that would apply to members of our group.

Double claims to be skeptical of these "non-realist" interpretations of reasonableness, including appeals to reflective equilibrium. But it is not clear why he is skeptical. We certainly employ interpretations of reasonableness in other areas of inquiry where there are no objective or universally true answers. Consider the way we evaluate literature. We might inquire about the criteria that must be satisfied in order for a novel to be called "great." It is true that (1) our considered judgments ultimately boil down to attitudes which, strictly speaking, have no truth values; and (2) that a universal convergence of these considered judgments is likely not forthcoming. Yet we do not throw up our hands and claim that all evaluative judgments are equally reasonable, or that all methods of approaching the question are equally reasonable. The only conclusion to which (1) and (2) commit us is that our verdict will not reflect an objective or universal truth. The same reasoning, I believe, can apply to the question of moral responsibility, even if metaskepticism or free will subjectivism is true.

This concludes my discussion contrasting metaskepticism with other non-traditional positions concerning moral responsibility. In what follows, I will consider how my position might affect issues of social policy and then I will lay out a framework for regarding moral responsibility, given the truth of metaskepticism.

SOCIAL AND POLITICAL IMPLICATIONS OF METASKEPTICISM

When I began writing this book, I had the rather grandiose idea that an entire chapter would be devoted to examining the implications of metaskepticism for foreign policy and criminal justice. I soon realized that these issues are manifold and complex and involve entirely different literatures than the ones I have been examining. My aspirations are now considerably more humble. I will not attempt a detailed analysis of how the truth of metaskepticism would affect theories of punishment and foreign engagement. Rather, I hope to raise some questions that are worth exploring in light of the evidence and arguments offered in the first part of this book.

Rhetoric that accompanies military intervention in the affairs of other countries often involves appeals to principles of autonomy, responsibility, and justice. Some have justified the invasion of Iraq as fulfilling a moral imperative to spread democratic values and the ideals of individual responsibility. Colonialist Western governments have offered similar justifications for hundreds of years. The truth of metaskepticism would rule out this type of justification, since there is no moral imperative to spread principles of autonomy and responsibility to areas where they would not be appropriate. It would be exceptionally naïve, however, to believe that a commitment to these principles is the true motivation behind acts of military expansion and intervention. So, while the metaskeptical thesis can undermine the *rhetoric* surrounding military expansion, it is less clear what effect it would have on the real reasons that governments pursue such expansion.

On a more practical level, the variation in perspectives about autonomy, responsibility, and justice has important implications for the ways in which governments engage in campaigns abroad. Some members of the U.S. military are beginning to recognize this (as they did during the war with Japan when they commissioned Ruth Benedict to conduct a study of Japanese values). Former Army Major William McCallister, now a consultant for the Marines, has argued that military policies in Iraq do not reflect an adequate understanding of cultural norms. According to McCallister, the concepts of shame and honor are as important to the Iraqis as land or water. They form the moral currency of the country (McCallister 2005). He attributes our unpopularity with Iraqi tribes in large part to our failure to understand this aspect of their society. Similar observations about the role of honor have been made about all the countries in that region. Thanks in large part to McCallister's efforts, the U.S. Army in 2006 released a 125-page handbook entitled *Through the Lens of Cultural Awareness: A Primer for US Armed Forces Deploying to Arab and Middle Eastern Countries*. This is clearly a step in the right direction. In order to shape policies properly, we need a comprehensive analysis of the role that honor plays in these countries and of the role that individual moral responsibility may *not* play. Once alerted to differences in ethical perspectives, we are less likely to expect people in honor cultures to immediately embrace American notions of justice. Certainly, appreciating these cultural differences would give soldiers and policymakers a more complete understanding of the moral motivations of Middle Easterners.

The same line of thinking applies to non-military policies that aim to influence the political structures of other cultures. Lee Kuan Yew, Prime Minister and then Senior Minister of Singapore from 1965 to 2004 has led a fascinating campaign criticizing the imperialism of Western governments. Lee, like Gomperz, claims that Western principles of individual liberty and responsibility emerge from a distinct religious and philosophical tradition; namely, the works of Locke and Kant—yet we mistake these principles for universal truths that everyone must accept. In an interview with Fareed Zakaria, Lee argued that Americans have turned the inviolability of the individual into dogma. Yet East Asian cultures do not conceive of their society in the same way:

> The fundamental difference between Western concepts of society and government and East Asian concepts . . . is that Eastern societies believe that the individual exists in the context of his family. He is not pristine and separate. The family is part of the extended family, and then friends and the wider society. (Zakaria and Lee, 1994 online interview)

Lee believes these differences indicate that a single political model cannot function in all cultures. He recognizes the virtues of the Western emphasis on individual liberty but claims that it would not be effective in his own society. When asked what is wrong with the American system, he replies: "It is not my business to tell people what's wrong with their system. It is my business to tell people not to foist their system indiscriminately on societies in which it will not work." One may certainly question whether these considerations can justify some of Singapore's more repressive policies. But Lee's claims about the tendency to mistake culturally and historically local perspectives for necessary universal truths are consistent with the arguments developed in Part One.

The metaskeptical thesis also raises deep philosophical questions about the justification for punishment. Criminal justice in America is in part grounded in abstract retributive principles that involve a strong notion of individual moral desert.[6] The research suggests, however, that certain principles, such as the principles of "positive retribution" (the view that culpable offenders *should* be punished) and "negative retribution" (the view that *only* culpable offenders should be punished), are not as universally held as is commonly supposed. These retributive concepts will likely strike an intuitive chord with members of non-honor groups; they are far less likely to do so in honor cultures. Criminal justice in America also functions to sever the connection between the victim's feelings and the amount of blame and punishment assigned to the offender. Members of honor cultures likely find the commitment to total impartiality and "blind justice" extremely unsatisfying. (Daly and Wilson 1988; Miller 2006; and recall Anthony James's reaction to the incarceration of his brother's murderer and the Albanian response to third-party punishment.) Indeed, on this point, members of non-honor cultures might agree, although less emphatically. This is not to say that victims should decide verdicts and determine sentences, or that they should handle their own business in the street. But greater sensitivity to variation may yield a balanced view about the relationship between justice and the victim. Indeed, some organizations, such as "JUST Alternatives" and their "victim-offender dialogue program," have been trying to move in this direction. At a more abstract level, the metaskeptical thesis raises the concern that we might be punishing criminals according to principles that (a) cannot be universally justified, and (b) are not shared by individuals in some groups throughout the United States.

Of course, all of these implications require extensive analysis, and metaskepticism is best thought of as only a point of departure in this process. I do hope, however, that my remarks have been sufficient to show that the questions raised by metaskeptical arguments are worth exploring in greater depth. In the next two chapters and the remainder of this one, I will turn away from societal implications and examine the implications of metaskepticism for the individual.

A Metaskeptical Approach to Moral Responsibility

In my critique of Double's view, I claimed that even if metaskepticism or some form of subjectivism is true, there are nonetheless reasonable and unreasonable ways to approach the issue of responsibility. The method of reflective equilibrium is unlikely to produce universally true conditions of moral responsibility, but it does provide us with a way to determine the conditions for moral responsibility that best reflect *our own* core values and attitudes.

How might this play out in practice? Let me use myself as an example. I have always found hard incompatibilism and other first-order skeptical positions compelling. As a metaphysical matter, I am convinced that no one can be ultimately responsible for any part of his or her character. I find the TNR principle intuitively appealing when considered abstractly, and I agree with Pereboom (2001) that it best accounts for my intuitions in particular cases like those in the four-case argument. At the same time, I find the hard incompatibilist conclusion—the claim

that no one can be morally responsible for his or her behavior—
difficult to accept as well. And when I imagine a case in which
someone deliberately and intentionally hurts a member of my
family, my commitment to the TNR principle loses virtually all
of its force. I am therefore faced with an inconsistency in my
own attitudes about responsibility, one that can only be resolved
by something like reflective equilibrium.

One might immediately suppose that the psychological difficulty of accepting a particular conclusion is not relevant to the
question of whether we ought to accept that conclusion or
whether it is true. If one accepts the premises of an argument,
one has to accept the conclusion, however counterintuitive it
might seem. But this objection does not seem to apply in cases
where acceptance of the premises depends on intuitive agreement. Pereboom himself makes this observation in his critique
of Haji's (1999, 2002) argument for the incompatibility of determinism and morally wrong actions. Pereboom acknowledges
the intuitive force of Haji's principles, but writes:

> The degree to which Haji's conclusions are unintuitive
> must be weighed against how unintuitive it is to reject one
> or more of his premises. . . . If the components of the the-
> ory derived from these principles conform to our intu-
> itions, that would provide theoretical support for them.
> But if such derived components do not conform to our in-
> tuitions, that would to some extent disconfirm these prin-
> ciples. I don't see how a principle's being an axiom in a
> moral theory would immunize it from such disconfirm-
> ing pressures. (Pereboom 2001, 144–45)

According to Pereboom, the unintuitiveness of Haji's conclusion—"nothing in determined worlds is right, wrong, and
obligatory"—places "disconfirming pressure" on the premises

that lead to it. Pereboom writes that were we to learn that determinism was true, it would seem "arbitrary to privilege absolutely [Haji's premises] over the claim that judgments of moral obligation are sometimes true" (Pereboom 2001, 146). Pereboom does not indicate precisely how we are to resolve this battle of conflicting intuitions, but it seems clear that he is endorsing something like reflective equilibrium as a means to a final verdict.

In my view (which I develop in Sommers 2009b), the hard incompatibilist argument is vulnerable to the same line of attack that Pereboom employs against Haji. The unintuitiveness of the hard incompatibilist conclusion puts "disconfirming pressure" on the key incompatibilist premise—namely, the TNR principle. One of Pereboom's reasons for re-examining his intuitive acceptance of the key principles in Haji's argument is that the conclusion "has the [unintuitive] consequence . . . that nothing Hitler ever did was wrong." No less hard to swallow is the hard incompatibilist conclusion that Hitler did not deserve blame or punishment for anything he ever did. It seems just as arbitrary to "privilege absolutely" the TNR principle over the belief that people like Hitler can deserve blame. The bottom line is that accepting hard incompatibilism requires more than a belief in the intuitive plausibility of the TNR principle. One must in addition show that the hard incompatibilist conclusion does not place so much "disconfirming pressure" on the TNR principle that we have reason to reject it in spite of its intuitive plausibility. Since our intuitions ultimately ground TNR, it seems that the method of wide reflective equilibrium is the best way, and likely the only way, to decide which beliefs about responsibility it is more reasonable to accept. And this is true even for those (like me) who think that a proper application of this method will not lead to the same conclusions for everyone.

So then, how precisely should we sort out our various intu-itions about the conditions for moral responsibility? I offer some factors to consider.

1. What is the strength of the intuition? How difficult psychologically would it be to give it up?
2. How well does the intuition cohere with other well-justified beliefs, moral and non-moral?
3. Can the intuition be "explained away" or debunked?
4. What is the pragmatic value of the intuition?

Some of these factors turn on matters of empirical fact and apply to everyone. Others relate only to our personal circumstances and temperament. Metaskepticism rules out universal agree-ment on these judgments, but there are many possible outcomes, ranging from agreement within large "intuition groups" (Mallon et al. 2009) whose members share core intuitions and norms, to an extreme subjectivism in which the judgments of a particular individual may change from day to day or year to year.

In the final two chapters, I will provide a tentative and often programmatic exploration of these factors for members of my "intuition group"—that is, members whose "starting" intuitions about responsibility resemble my own. Chapter 6 examines the "all-things-considered" cases for libertarianism and compatibil-ism. And chapter 7 considers what it would mean to deny moral responsibility in the manner of the first-order skeptic or hard incompatibilist.

CHAPTER SIX

A Metaskeptical Analysis of Libertarianism and Compatibilism

From the first time I encountered the problem of free will in college, it struck me that a clear-eyed view of free will and moral responsibility demanded some form of nihilism. Libertarianism seemed delusional, and compatibilism seemed in bad faith. Hence I threw my lot in with philosophers like Paul d'Holbach, Galen Strawson, and Derk Pereboom who conclude that no one is truly morally responsible. But after two decades of self-identifying as a nihilist, it occurred to me that I had continued to treat my friends, colleagues, and acquaintances as morally responsible. Hardly ever did I call on my philosophical views to excuse people's actions.

—Shaun Nichols, "After Incompatibilism"

COMPETING BELIEFS

Like Shaun Nichols, I have always found the arguments for nihilism or skepticism compelling. The TNR principle, which is at the heart of these arguments, seems to me to reflect a basic principle of fairness. Yet like Nichols I hold myself morally responsible all the time. I feel that I deserve blame for my bad actions and praise for good actions and accomplishments. I also commonly hold other people morally responsible—my family, friends, criminals, and (perhaps especially) athletes who are connected in any way to Boston sports.[1] At the gut level, then, I find the belief that people can be morally responsible (PMR henceforth) to be intuitively compelling as well. Of course, the TNR and PMR beliefs are not inconsistent on their own. The inconsistency arises only for those who agree with Nichols that libertarianism is "delusional" or at any rate false. Indeed, the appeal of libertarianism is precisely that it allows us to retain two intuitively compelling beliefs, one about the conditions of moral responsibility (TNR) and the other that people are capable of being morally responsible (PMR).

So metaskeptics have at least three options when trying to determine the most reasonable all-things-considered position about responsibility. Compatibilism allows us to regard ourselves and others as morally responsible agents, though at the cost of rejecting the highly intuitive TNR principle. Nihilism allows us to retain TNR, but at the cost of denying the highly intuitive belief that people can be morally responsible. Finally, there is libertarianism, which allows us to accept both TNR and PMR, but at the price of some thorny empirical and theoretical problems that will be discussed below. In this chapter I will evaluate the cases for libertarianism and compatibilism for people who share my core starting intuitions about the conditions of moral responsibility. In the next chapter, I will consider the case for nihilism or eliminativism. The goal of these final two chapters is not to arrive at a decisive conclusion (a good thing because I do not) but rather to lay out and apply the method metaskeptics can employ for arriving at all-things-considered responsibility judgments. Readers may apply the same method and arrive at a different verdict. Indeed, the conclusions generated by this method will almost certainly vary from culture to culture and possibly from person to person. Nevertheless, the method itself is something that can be adopted universally as a means of identifying the most reasonable position for people in each "intuition group" to embrace.

The Case for Libertarianism

The criticisms that have been directed at libertarianism are well known and compelling. The event-causal varieties (e.g., Kane 1996 or Ekstrom 2000), have little if anything in the way of empirical support (Vargas 2007). Agent-causal varieties rely on metaphysical views that are incoherent at worst, empirically dubious at best. More damaging to the view is that even when one grants libertarians their metaphysics, it remains unclear how their accounts can provide agents with the right kind of control for moral responsibility. For these reasons, like Nichols, I have never found libertarianism to be a serious contender in the free will and moral responsibility debate. Daniel Speak, however, has identified a controversial assumption that lurks behind these criticisms. He writes: "Opponents of libertarianism make their arguments on the assumption that moral and pragmatic considerations about the value of libertarian agency are strictly irrelevant to its philosophical assessment" (Speak 2004, 353). And he goes on to provide compelling reasons to doubt this assumption, concluding that "the case for libertarianism may very well stand or fall with an overall assessment of its importance to human life (moral and otherwise)" (353). Pointing to the recent "pragmatic encroachment" (Jonathan Kvanvig's term) into issues of epistemic justification in general, Speak argues for an axiological approach to free will and moral responsibility. His methodological conclusions are similar to my own as described in chapter 5: We should try to arrive at "all-things-considered" judgments about the condition for free will and moral responsibility, judgments that incorporate *values* as well as facts. The pragmatic or moral reasons for accepting libertarianism may be significant enough to outweigh evidentiary or theoretical factors that count against the position.

I agree with Speak that this outcome cannot be dismissed out of hand.[2] With this in mind, let us examine some considerations that seem to favor libertarian theories of free will and moral responsibility.

The Phenomenological Fit

One virtue of libertarianism is that it seems to describe the phenomenology of agency and responsibility more effectively than competing positions. As Galen Strawson (a skeptic) writes:

> We are, in the most ordinary situations of choice, unable not to think that we will be truly or absolutely responsible for our choice, whatever we choose. Our natural thought may be expressed as follows: even if my character is indeed just something given (a product of heredity and environment or whatever), I am still able to choose (and hence act) completely freely and truly responsibly, given how I now am and what I now know; this is so whatever else is the case—determinism or no determinism. (Strawson 1986, 116)

Strawson gives a vivid description of this phenomenology in the following example: Imagine, he writes, that it is Christmas Eve and you are going to buy a bottle of scotch with your last twenty-dollar bill. Right outside the liquor store, there is a beggar who is clearly in need. You must decide now whether to spend your money on the scotch, or give it to the beggar.

You stop, and it seems quite clear to you — it surely *is* quite clear to you — that it is *entirely up to you* what you do next — in such a way that you will have deep moral responsibility for what you do, whatever you do. The situation is in fact utterly clear: you can put the money into the beggar's tin or you can go in and buy the scotch. You're not only completely, radically free to choose in this situation. You're not free not to choose. That's how it feels. (1986, *x* [preface])

Strawson is right, I believe, that libertarianism best captures the subjective experience of moral deliberation, a point that must count in its favor. Some libertarians have made the much stronger claim that belief in libertarian free will is *required* in order for us to believe that we engage in rational deliberation. According to this view, when we deliberate we must assume (a) that there are two possible outcomes, and (b) that we have the power to bring about either one of them. As Van Inwagen (1983, 155) writes:

If someone deliberates about whether to do A or to do B, it follows that his behavior manifests a belief that it is *possible* for him to do A—that he *can* do A, that he has it within his power to do A—and a belief that it is possible for him to do B.

If this view is correct, the cost of denying libertarianism would indeed be enormous. In order to consistently deny libertarian free will I would have to deny, in addition, that I deliberate—and the belief that I deliberate is close to non-negotiable. But Van Inwagen is mistaken on this point. For while it does feel as though there are two metaphysically open alternatives when I deliberate, it does not feel *impossible* that I am determined to

deliberate in a particular way and to arrive at a particular conclusion. Indeed, this does not even seem unlikely. Furthermore,
the possibility that my deliberation is determined does not
make it seem pointless, since the deliberation would still play a
causal role in determining the outcome. To think otherwise
confuses determinism with fatalism.

So what precisely do we need to believe in order to engage in
rational deliberation? Pereboom (2008) lays out two conditions
both of which are consistent with the truth of determinism and
thus with the denial of libertarian free will. First, there must be
epistemic openness: that is, we must not know the outcome of
our deliberation in advance. Second, we must believe that the
deliberation is, under normal conditions, *efficacious*—that the
final choice will be causally influenced by the deliberation process. Pereboom's argument for the sufficiency of these conditions is in my view decisive. Here is an example from my own
past (and readers may think back to some episode in their own
lives that required deliberation): About ten years ago, I faced a
decision about whether to attend a graduate program in philosophy or to continue my so-called career as a freelance writer.
At the time, I had no idea which choice I would end up making.
I also believed (correctly) that my deliberations would have
causal influence over the final verdict, whatever that turned out
to be. So the act of deliberating made perfect sense. Yet even
during the deliberation process, it did not seem implausible that
the outcome was inevitable. And after the decision was made, as
I was reflecting back on the process, it seemed to me rather
likely that the deliberation occurred in a deterministic fashion.
There is a *feeling* of metaphysical openness, but it is mostly con-
fined to the present moment. At no point in the process did the
possibility of determinism or the lack of libertarian free will un-

dermine my belief that the deliberation was rational, genuine, and effective.

Objective Worth

Another factor to be considered is the connection between libertarianism and what Kane (1996) calls "objective worth." If objective worth is important to us, and it is incompatible with non-libertarian accounts of free will and responsibility, then we would have a powerful pragmatic reason to accept libertarianism, all things considered. So in this section I try to shed light on three questions:

1. What is objective worth?
2. Is objective worth so defined valuable or important?
3. Is objective worth only compatible with libertarian conceptions of free will and responsibility?

(1) WHAT IS OBJECTIVE WORTH?

Kane illustrates the notion of objective worth with the story of Alan the artist. Alan is depressed because no one appreciates his paintings. To cheer him up, a rich friend of Alan's arranges to have his paintings purchased at an art gallery for $10,000 apiece. Alan assumes that his work is finally receiving the critical and popular recognition he feels it deserves, and so he feels much better. Kane then asks us to image two worlds. In the first, Alan is mistaken about the merit of his paintings—his rich friend has tricked him into thinking he is a great artist and that he is being recognized as one. In the second, Alan's beliefs about his talent are correct. The rich friend has not deceived him to lift his spirits, he merely provided the necessary impetus for others to appreciate him. In both worlds, "Alan dies happily believing he is a great artist, though only in the second was his belief correct" (Kane 1996, 97). [3]

The key question, then, is whether it would make any difference to Alan which of these worlds he belonged to. According to Kane, if we agree that there is an important difference in value for Alan in the two worlds, then we must endorse a notion of objective worth.

Since Alan's subjective experiences would be identical in both worlds, any difference in their value must consist in something over and above the feelings of happiness he experiences from the belief that he is a great artist. There is some value, then, in Alan's belief being *true* and his feeling of happiness being warranted.

(2) IS OBJECTIVE WORTH VALUABLE?

Compatibilists and skeptics about responsibility would likely agree that this type of objective worth is valuable. As Kane writes, there is something demeaning about being praised for works that are in reality worthless—even if we never know that we were being deceived. The controversy, then, focuses on the answer to the final question:

(3) IS OBJECTIVE WORTH ONLY COMPATIBLE WITH
LIBERTARIAN CONCEPTIONS OF FREE WILL AND MR?

According to Kane, libertarian free will, the capacity to be ultimately responsible for our characters, is "of a piece" with this notion of objective worth:

> If, like Alan, we think that the objective worth of our acts or accomplishments is something valuable over and above the felt satisfaction the acts have or bring, then I suggest that we will be inclined to think that a freedom requiring

ultimate responsibility is valuable over and above compatibilist freedoms from coercion, compulsion, and oppres-
sion. . . . Such freedoms would be enough, if we did not
care in addition, like Alan, about more than what pleases
us—namely, if we did not care in addition about our "worthiness" or "deservingness" to be pleased. Are our acts or
deeds, our accomplishments and we ourselves, objectively
worthy of recognition, respect, love, or praise, as Alan
wished for his paintings or as he might wish for himself?
It is this concern for the objective desert of our deeds and
characters that leads naturally to a concern about whether
those deeds and characters have their ultimate sources in
us rather than in someone or something else (fate or God,
genes or environment, social conditioning or behavioral
controllers). Do they ultimately redound to us or not? The
answer to this question does not have to do merely with
subjective happiness, but with the objective worth of our
selves and our lives. (97–98)

Here Kane attempts to draw an analogy between Alan's paintings and our actions and character. Just as Alan wants his paintings to be worthy, we want our actions and characters, our
selves, to be truly worthy of respect, recognition, and praise.

Even when we grant Kane our desire for worthiness, however, there still seems to be a gap in how that is connected with
libertarian free will. Mele (1999) points out correctly that compatibilists may have an equally strong preference to live in an
objectively worthy world. About Kane's example of Alan, he
writes:

A compatibilist can reasonably prefer actually being a
great artist and having the associated feelings and experiences of success to having the same feelings and experi-

ences while falsely believing himself to be a great artist. He can prefer that these qualitative states are grounded in his excellent work and that he not be radically deceived about himself. (103)

Indeed, in Kane's example of the objectively worthy world, nothing required that Alan be the ultimate source of his talent and abilities as a painter. This world only required that Alan's paintings actually be of high quality. Kane's remark that concern for objective worth leads us "naturally" to a concern about "whether those deeds and characters have their ultimate sources in us rather than in someone or something else" seems unmotivated by his own example. Alan does not indicate any concern about whether his talents and abilities have their ultimate source in him. Why should this be such a concern for us?

Mele's objection can be taken further. Objective worth does not even seem dependent on a *compatibilist* notion of responsibility. Consider the case of someone who is concerned with the objective worth of his ability (like Alan), but who does not presume himself to be responsible for that ability *in any way*:

Joe the naturally funny guy. Joe has the talent to make people around him laugh heartily. He is able to find the humor in a conversation or situation as it's happening, and the right words come into his head quickly enough for him to articulate them. Irreverence, wit, and originality come naturally to Joe. He takes pride in this aspect of his character—it is an appealing quality, part of the reason he is well liked by his friends and family. Nevertheless, it is not an aspect of Joe's character for which he considers himself responsible *in any way*. He does not know what combination of causes produced his sense of humor—family, genes, upbringing—but he is certain that the source is not *him* in the libertarian sense. What is more, Joe has not made a higher-level endorsement of a decision to be funny, he has not responded to reasons in favor of making jokes. He has not studied or worked hard to cultivate his wit. It requires little or no effort whatsoever. Joe, in other words, does not consider himself *responsible* for this aspect of his character in either the compatibilist or the libertarian sense. He sees it as a natural trait that he is lucky to have, like being physically attractive or having a photographic memory.

Now consider a world in which Joe has all the same beliefs about his wit, the same pride in being funny, the same sense of satisfaction every time one of his remarks provokes a round of hearty laughter. But in this world, Joe's wealthy father has paid the people around him to laugh at his jokes. In fact, Joe's remarks are not funny at all. They fail to capture the irony of a situation, they are often deeply offensive or too politically correct, sometimes both at once. But the actors around Joe never let on. Joe goes to his grave believing himself to be as funny as Peter Sellers in his prime.

In this case, as in Alan's, we can agree that there is value to being in the first world, the one in which Joe is genuinely funny. There is objective worth in having a good sense of humor over and above the subjective feelings of happiness and satisfaction that come with it. But the objective worth of this quality is disconnected from the need to be responsible for the quality in any way at all, let alone the need for it to have its "ultimate source in us rather than in someone or something else." Joe is certain that he is not responsible for the gift. But this does not affect the value he places on the quality's authenticity. The only thing that could undermine the authenticity of his ability would be the discovery that he is in fact not funny. Objective worth, then, does not appear to be "of a piece" with ultimate responsibility or indeed responsibility of any kind.

The Moral Benefits of Libertarianism

Though not a libertarian himself, Smilansky's (2000) "illusion-ism" provides the axiological or pragmatic case for libertarian-ism with additional ammunition. Smilansky argues that we should retain the illusion of libertarian free will due to its moral importance. Two of his worries are pragmatic in nature. First, he argues that knowing in advance that we will not be ultimately responsible for future actions would undermine our motivation to refrain from wrongdoing. Smilansky calls this the "present danger of the future retrospective excuse." The second and re-lated "danger of worthlessness" posits that our motivation to perform morally worthy actions will be harmed by the knowl-edge that our responsibility will be of the "significantly shal-lower compatibilist variety" (Smilansky 2000, 53).

Smilansky's claims are based on some controversial assump-tions about the nature of moral motivation, and, until recently, there was no empirical evidence to support his pessimistic claims. This changed with a study conducted by Vohs and Schooler (2008). Subjects in the study were divided into two groups. In the first condition, subjects read a passage from Fran-cis Crick's *The Astonishing Hypothesis* stating that scientists have denounced the notion of free will. In the second condition, sub-jects read a different excerpt from Crick's book that did not refer to free will. The authors then gave the subjects cognitive tasks that featured opportunities to cheat, including one where they could pocket some extra money for doing so. The authors pre-dicted that the subjects who had read the denunciation of free will would be more likely to cheat on their tasks, and the results supported the prediction. Vohs and Schooler conclude their paper by asking: "Does the belief that forces outside the self determine behavior drain the motivation to resist the temptation to cheat, inducing a "why bother" mentality? . . . Or perhaps denying free will simply provide the ultimate excuse to behave as one likes" (54).[4]

Vohs and Schooler do not make the distinction between compatibilist and libertarian free will; rather, they assume that free will must be of the libertarian variety and their scenarios are designed to challenge the existence of libertarian free will in the minds of their subjects. Thus, their studies provide an important challenge both to "happy hard determinists" (Smilansky's term) and to compatibilists who argue that denying libertarianism would have either beneficial or neutral implications for human beings as a whole. But is the challenge successful? I do not believe so. For one thing, our behavior just after hearing that a cherished belief is false may have little or no bearing on how we would act after further reflection.[5] The authors cite no studies that document such a correlation. A religious person may experience some moral lapses just after having his faith challenged, but soon after come to realize that his values did not depend on his belief in God after all. The debate over the moral implications of denying libertarian free will focuses on long term effects. Vohs and Schooler may merely have shown that people should not lose their belief in libertarian free will fifteen minutes before they submit their tax return.

The relevant experiment would be one that tested the motivations of people who have denied libertarian free will and moral responsibility for long periods. Unfortunately, the pool of subjects for such an experiment is small, so Smilansky is limited to hypothetical examples. He raises a concern, for example, about the moral motivations of heroes facing situations of grave risk. He writes:

Think about someone on the eve of a mission which he knows is more likely than not to cost him his life: say, being parachuted into al-Qaida territory in Afghanistan, or being sent to infiltrate the Mafia. Do we not think that such a person is affected by what he thinks others will think and feel about his or her actions? That he will be honored by his colleagues, or respected by the public, or even forever hero-worshipped by his young nephew, in a real, robust way? A robust way assumes that it was, in fact, in a strong sense up to him not to do this, and that hence he is deserving of our appreciation (not only because to do so makes good utilitarian sense), and has through his choice acquired high moral value. (Smilansky 2010, 197)

According to Smilansky, it is crucial that these courageous heroes believe that they have done something that most people would not have done and that they themselves could have chosen not to do. And the heroes must also believe that other people believe this about them as well. (That is what will make them heroes in the eyes of the others.) If their heroism is just an "unfolding of the given," and they and other people know this, they will lack sufficient motivation for undergoing serious risk.

In a speculative case like this, argument can take us only so far. Not surprisingly, I see no connection between the heroes' motivations and their belief in libertarian free will. The notion that determinism could undermine their heroism strikes me as bizarre. A hero is a hero. They do things that most people cannot do. We do not find beautiful men and women any less attractive because we know that their appearance is not in a deep sense up to them. The desire to achieve a moral end is all the motivation that a moral hero needs. Consider people like Martin Luther King, Jr., or Mahatma Gandhi. Do we imagine that they performed heroic actions so that they could deserve praise and appreciation? The most obvious motivation for battling injustice is to end injustice. There is of course room for cynicism about the real causes of moral heroism, but we can at least say this: There is *no evidence whatsoever* that a belief in libertarian free will and moral responsibility played even the slightest role in motivating people like King, Gandhi, or other, less celebrated heroes who risk their lives to help others. As Franco and Zimbardo (2006, 33) note, "The first response of many people who are called heroes is to deny their own uniqueness with statements such as, 'I am not a hero; anyone in the same situation would have done what I did,' or, 'I just did what needed to be done.'" This could of course be false modesty on their part. But there is no reason to think that it is, nor is there any reason to think that their heroic behavior was motivated *even in part* by the knowledge that it would render them praiseworthy in the ultimate libertarian sense.

In addition to his pragmatic concerns about motivation, Smilansky, like Kane, argues that the *real moral value* of moral heroism is essentially connected to the ultimate responsibility of the hero. He writes:

True *appreciation,* deeply *attributing* matters to someone in a sense that will make him worthy, is impossible if we regard him and his efforts as merely determined products. . . . From the ultimate perspective, all people, whatever their efforts and sacrifices are morally equal: i.e., there cannot be any means of generating "real" moral value. . . . there is a sense in which our notion of moral self-respect, which is intimately connected with our view of choices, actions, and achievements, withers when we accept the ultimate perspective. From the latter any sense of moral achievement disappears, as even the actions of the "moral hero" are simply an unfolding of what he happens to be. *No matter how devoted he has been, how much effort he has put in, how many tears he has shed, how many sacrifices he has willingly suffered.* (Smilansky 2000, 163, his italics)

These claims strikes me as implausible even in the abstract—a kind of Kantianism gone wild—and when applied to concrete cases, they become even more implausible. Consider a holocaust survivor who owes her life to the courage of a family that risked being captured by the SS in order to shelter her. Imagine that she later became convinced that determinism was true. Would she no longer find real moral value in the family's actions? Would she no longer truly appreciate them? As a matter of psychological fact, the answer is almost certainly no. And the woman's psychology is indeed the relevant factor. Appreciation, true appreciation, is an affective response. If, after due reflection, the determinist holocaust survivor still feels appreciation, if she still finds "real value" in the actions of the family that sheltered her, then the actions have value—at least, in the context of the present discussion, which is after all focused on pragmatic or axiological concerns. The same goes for the self-respect of the members of the family. If they sense deep appreciation on the part of people they helped, if they believe that their actions served a worthy purpose, they will likely feel a deep sense of self-respect, in spite of not being the ultimate source of their actions.

THE CASE AGAINST LIBERTARIANISM

In the preceding discussion we examined several possible axiological or pragmatic benefits of retaining a belief in libertarian free will and moral responsibility. I argued that in each case the benefits were not all they were cracked up to be. In this section I examine the costs of a adopting a belief in libertarianism and argue that the costs, when taken together, weigh against an all-things-considered endorsement of libertarianism.

The Difficulty of Articulation

Much of the debate in the free will literature about libertarianism concerns the intelligibility or coherence of the position. Nagel (1979), Strawson (1986), and Wolf (1990), among many others, argue that the type of free will and ultimate responsibility endorsed by the libertarian is logically impossible, while Pereboom (2001), Mele (1995), Kane (1996), and O'Connor (2000) have defended the position's coherence. What is uncontroversial is the *difficulty* of articulating precisely how the falsity of determinism provides us with the kind of ultimate responsibility the libertarian treasures. This difficulty has led to some diminished expectations on the part of many libertarians. Wiggins, for example, writes:

> One of the many reasons I believe why philosophy falls short of a satisfying solution to the problem of freedom is that we still cannot refer to an unflawed statement of libertarianism. Perhaps libertarianism is, in the last analysis, untenable. But if we are to salvage its insights we need to know what is the *least unreasonable* statement the position can be given. (1973, 33, my italics)

Kane (1996, 106) cites this passage as in line with his own project. "Can we show that such [libertarian] freedom is coherent," he asks, "and give a clearer account of it than libertarians have offered in the past, an account that might show how such a freedom could exist in the natural order?" Libertarian ambition reaches its nadir in Van Inwagen's (1983, 2000) "mind argument" *against* indeterministic free will. Since the consequence argument is supposed to rule out the possibility of deterministic free will, one might expect Van Inwagen to become a skeptic. Instead, he concludes that free will undeniably exists but "remains a mystery."

If we are to embrace libertarianism, it appears that the most we can hope for is an account that *could* exist in the natural order, and offers the "least unreasonable" explanation for how indeterminism adds anything to compatibilist accounts of responsible agency. I cannot think of another theory, in any area, that we would even consider accepting on such a flimsy basis. The difficulty of articulation, then, counts as a significant cost to accepting libertarian free will.

Empirical Implausibility

Of all the theories of moral responsibility, libertarianism is the most empirically demanding. As Vargas (2007) notes, it is not enough that the world contain indeterministic events. The burden of libertarianism "is that it must hold that the indeterminism shows up at particular times and places" (142). The evidence that this occurs is not just lacking, it is non-existent:

> The main problem concerning the empirical plausibility of this view is that *there are no accepted scientific models of indeterministic brain events.* Indeed, virtually all brain science proceeds on the supposition of thoroughly deterministic explanations of the operations of the mind, and what evidence there is weighs against indeterministic interpretations of brain phenomena. (Vargas 2007, 144)

Of course, brain science *could* one day vindicate an account like Kane's. But the bare possibility that libertarianism could conceivably enjoy empirical support in the future is not enough. In other areas of our epistemic lives, we resist accepting beliefs that we have no positive reason to believe are true. This is a core epistemic principle, at least for naturalists—and for non-naturalists, too, in most areas of their lives. Rejecting this principle in order to retain our belief in libertarian free will would fracture our epistemology. The pragmatic considerations in favor of the belief would have to be overwhelming to offset this cost.

Moral Hardness

These epistemic costs raise troubling moral issues as well. If we accept libertarianism, we can then hold people ultimately responsible for their behavior. We believe they can deserve blame and punishment, independent of consequentialist considerations. Given that we lack epistemic justification for this belief, we are open to the charge of what Double (2002) terms "moral hardness." He notes that libertarians use the assignment of moral responsibility to turn otherwise immoral treatment into "just-deserts goods." Thus, even if there were pragmatic value in accepting libertarianism from our own perspective, we would still have to consider the moral cost to others. Vargas (2007, 140) makes a similar point:

> Imagine a criminal asking you why he should be made to serve for a longer period of time, when the only answer appeals to a conception of agency *which has no evidence in its favor.* . . . It is the wrong kind of faith to suppose that the moral acceptability of our denying clearly valuable things to these agents is justified or justifiable. It matters whether there is evidence that suggests we are libertarian agents, and so we must do better than to believe it on faith.

To Vargas's and Double's points, I would add that not only is there no evidence for libertarian free will and responsibility, but there is no clear way to articulate what it would be if it did exist or how it might justify the criminal's blameworthiness and punishment. Imagine a libertarian who, following Van Inwagen, must explain to the criminal that the type of agency that justifies his punishment is incoherent and therefore "a mystery." The acceptance of libertarianism on such flimsy grounds is therefore inconsistent with a moral principle that requires a great deal of epistemic justification before permitting the mistreatment or harm of others.

Conclusion: An All-Things-Considered Rejection of Libertarianism

When we employ the above considerations in generating all-things-considered judgments, the case for libertarianism turns out to be pretty weak. On the one hand, we can reject libertarianism and still believe in the effectiveness of deliberation and in the existence of objective and moral worth; on the other, accepting a belief in libertarian free will creates inconsistencies with core epistemic and moral principles that we apply in all other areas of our lives. In short, the axiological and pragmatic benefits of accepting libertarianism do not seem to offset the costs. Libertarianism is therefore not a viable all-things-considered conclusion—at least for people whose epistemic and moral commitments resemble my own.

THE CASE FOR COMPATIBILISM

Compatibilism about moral responsibility is both celebrated and mocked for its "best of both worlds" qualities. Compatibilists can be empirically sound naturalists and at the same time claim all of the practical and moral benefits cherished by the libertarian (with the exception of a metaphysically open future.[6]) The primary cost of compatibilism is that one has to reject the TNR principle. Compatibilists and nihilists tend to agree about relevant metaphysical and non-moral issues. Both accept that our actions are the result of factors that trace back beyond our control. Their disagreement is over whether it is fair or appropriate to hold agents morally responsible for such actions.

The debate between compatibilists and nihilists about moral responsibility, then, boils down to which of two intuitive beliefs they choose to reject: the TNR principle or the belief that people can be morally responsible (PMR). If the TNR principle has intuitive force (as it does for me), embracing compatibilism will require that we revise our concept of moral responsibility so that so that it can accommodate our lack of ultimate responsibility. The all-things-considered case for compatibilism then becomes equivalent to what Vargas (2007) calls "moderate revisionism" about moral responsibility. In order to highlight the contrast, I will henceforth refer to skeptical or hard incompatibilist or nihilist accounts as "eliminativism" about moral responsibility. (The difficulty in coming up with an acceptable name for this position is a significant pragmatic cost of adopting it.) In this section, I will offer a critical examination of the case for revisionist compatibilism, one that, as always, is restricted to members of my intuition group.

The Strength of Our Commitment to Moral Responsibility

Following Strawson (2003 [1962]), many contemporary compatibilists call attention to the strength of our commitment to moral responsibility and, in particular, to the reactive attitudes that are bound up with this commitment.[7] Strawson claims that the real question in the debate is whether the truth of determinism could cause us to reject our responsibility related attitudes. Strawson answers no: "We cannot, as it were, seriously envisage ourselves adopting a thoroughgoing objectivity of attitude to others as a result of the theoretical conviction of the truth of determinism" (Strawson 2003, 82). Strawson argues further that a commitment to the reactive attitudes entails a commitment to moral responsibility. If he is right, eliminativism is not option. It would require adopting "the objective attitude" on an exclusive basis, something that we are not psychologically capable of doing. And it cannot be rational to do what we are not capable of doing. Nichols (2007) refers to this strategy as the "insulationist move": our attitudes and practices related to moral responsibility are insulated from theoretical threats posed by incompatibilist arguments.

It is certainly true that we are deeply committed to seeing others and, especially, ourselves as morally responsible agents, and as appropriate candidates of attitudes like resentment. Indeed, as Strawson argues, it is hard even to imagine what it would be like to give up this belief in its entirety. But is the rejection of moral responsibility and its accompanying attitudes and practices *impossible*? I do not believe so. Both Bennett (1980) and Russell (1995) contrast the Strawsonian position with that of the Spinozist. The Spinozist does indeed try to take the objective attitude on an exclusive basis, and he does so precisely because of a general theoretical belief in determinism. True, we often *think* we are morally responsible, but this is only because we are ignorant of the causes of our behavior. Once we are aware of these causes, the Spinozist argues, our responsibility-presupposing attitudes fade away. As Stuart Hampshire writes in his

study of Spinoza, once the causes of a certain type of behavior
are understood,

> ... we do in fact cease to apply purely moral epithets to
> them as responsible agents. When the behavior now caus-
> ally explained is what was formerly regarded as morally
> wicked, we come to regard it as the symptom of a disease,
> curable, if at all, by the removal of its causes; expressions
> of moral disapproval come to seem useless and irrelevant.
> (Hampshire 1951, 158)

Now if determinism is true, the Spinozist goes on, then *every*
action has causes for which the agent is not morally responsible.
The only question is whether we can *identify* the causes of the
action, and this is a purely epistemic question that should have
no bearing on whether the agent actually deserves blame or
praise for that action. How many practicing Spinozists there are
in this world is an open question, but Spinoza himself may serve
as a counterexample to Strawson's insulationist claims. By most
accounts Spinoza was said to live pretty much in accordance
with his beliefs, showing little traces of resentment or bitterness
over the considerable injustices done to him. Many Buddhist
masters, too, are said to have banished emotions like resentment and hatred as a result of an understanding that the behavior of others is caused, and that the source of bad behavior is
ignorance. The most appropriate reaction, they feel, is compassion, just as one might feel compassion for a sick person. And
Charles Darwin expresses a similar view in his notebooks:

> This view [the denial of free will] should teach one pro-
> found humility, one deserves no credit for anything. (yet
> one takes it for beauty and good temper), nor ought one to
> blame others ... we must view a wicked man like a sickly

one. It would be more proper to pity than to hate & be disgusted."[8]

Darwin, Spinoza, and a Buddhist monk might not appear to have much in common, but one thing they do seem to share is a belief that claims about moral desert are inappropriate if our actions have causes for which we are not responsible. It seems, then, that theoretical concerns *can* have an effect on our reactive attitudes and responsibility practices. As Galen Strawson writes, "The roots of the incompatibilist intuition lie deep in the very reactive attitudes that are invoked to undercut it. The reactive attitudes enshrine the incompatibilist intuition" (1986, 89).

One might object that all known cultures have believed in the concept and importance of moral responsibility (even if there is variation concerning the conditions for its application). Indeed, my analysis in Part One supports this claim. None of my examples presented a culture that denied the existence of responsibility altogether. The universality of the commitment to moral responsibility seems to indicate that the concept plays a valuable and perhaps indispensible role in our social lives.

This is a serious objection to which I offer two tentative replies.[9] First, the importance of the responsibility concept in regulating the moral behavior of groups in the past does not entail its indispensability. It may be that present and future societies can flourish without the concept—especially if appropriate analogues are provided in its place. (See Pereboom (2001), Sommers (2007a), and the following chapter for a description of these analogues.) At one time, virtually all societies believed in the importance and truth of religion. Religious beliefs were intimately connected with moral norms and practices, and many predicted disaster if society at large were to lose its faith. But the doomsday scenarios have not come to pass in countries such as the Czech Republic where a large proportion of the citizenry have become atheists and agnostics. The same may be true for societies that give up their belief in desert-entailing moral responsibility. We will not know for sure until we have a concrete example.

My second reply concerns the scope of my ambitions in these two chapters. My goal is not to speculate about what would happen if an *entire society* retained or rejected their belief in moral responsibility. Rather, it is to examine the implications of the various positions for individuals. It is arguable that no society (especially in the West) will *ever* fully embrace the notion that we are not free and morally responsible. Powerful psychological and cultural forces push us to believe in the reality of these concepts, and most people lack the resources and the inclination to resist those forces. Particular individuals, on the other hand, can become committed nihilists at any time and endeavor to diminish the influence of responsibility-presupposing attitudes on their beliefs and behavior. This is why I focus on examples like Darwin and Spinoza—individuals whose theories caused them to deny free will and moral responsibility but who lived in societies where these concepts were, and still are, pervasive. Indeed, there is a real sense in which it would be inappropriate for me, as a metaskeptic, to be a missionary for a particular first-order position. Many people in my society may not belong to my intuition group—they may not share my core starting intuitions, and they could, therefore, arrive just as reasonably at a different final verdict.

In sum, I agree with Strawson and his followers that our intuitions and sentiments pull many of us in the direction of holding a person responsible when he meets appropriate compatibilist conditions. But another set of intuitions pulls us towards mitigation or exoneration once we see that factors beyond the agent's control are the ultimate cause of his or her action. A slew of recent studies in experimental philosophy suggest that we are deeply conflicted when it comes to our beliefs about moral responsibility. Factors such as emotional salience, concreteness, mood, psychological distance, and even the messiness of our surroundings can incline us in one direction or the other.[10] It seems, then, that we cannot make the case for compatibilism solely on the basis of our belief in moral responsibility or our commitment to responsibility-presupposing attitudes.

Can the TNR Intuition Be Explained Away?

The compatibilist at this point may argue that incompatibilist principles only seem plausible because of some mistaken assumptions about what they involve. Incompatibilist principles like TNR will lose their intuitive appeal once they are properly understood. Nahmias, Coates, and Kvaran (2007) and Nahmias and Murray (2010) have recently developed an "error theory" for incompatibilist judgments. According to these authors, many people who appear to have incompatibilist intuitions are interpreting determinism to involve the *bypassing* (or causal impotence) of desires and conscious deliberation. But this is a mistake, since deterministic or naturalistic accounts of human behavior do not entail that our desires and deliberation are causally impotent. The authors conclude that to the extent that we have them, incompatibilist intuitions can be traced to this mistake of confusing determinism with fatalism.

To support this interpretation, the authors developed two kinds of deterministic scenarios—one in which conscious deliberation is bypassed, and one in which it is not. The authors operate under the assumption that when the decision-making process is described mechanistically as neural processes and chemical reactions in the agent's brain, subjects tend to think that beliefs, desires, and reasoning are causally impotent. This assumption provides the key manipulation for the deterministic scenarios. In one condition, the agents' decision-making is described "in terms of neuroscientific, mechanistic processes (neuro scenarios)"; in the other, decision-making is described "in terms of psychological, intentional processes (psych scenarios)." The authors made three central predictions:

1. Most people will judge that determinism is *not* threatening to free will and moral responsibility if determinism is described in *non*mechanistic (psychological) terms.

2. Significantly more people will judge determinism to be threatening if determinism is described in mechanistic (neuroscientific) terms.

3. People will significantly increase their attributions of free will and moral responsibility [in both conditions] in response to descriptions of specific agents who perform bad acts in comparison to agents and actions described in abstract ways. (Nahmias et al. 2007, 221)

The results appear to offer significant support for their predictions. Subjects tended to give compatibilist responses in the abstract/psych condition but incompatibilist responses in the abstract/neuro condition. Neuroscientific descriptions of decision-making seem to be more of a threat to responsibility than psychological ones.

The authors' target is a study by Nichols and Knobe (2007) that offers support for the view that the "folk" have incompatibilist commitments. They object to Nichols and Knobe's description of determinism, which includes the claim that "given the past, each decision *has to happen* the way that it does." The "had to happen" language, according to Nahmias et al., leads subjects to think that the actions they perform will occur no matter what their desires, intentions, and reasons may incline them to do.

However, if Nahmias and colleagues have grounds to object to the "had to happen" language, incompatibilists can complain in turn that the authors' own description of the "psychological" condition does not make determinism sufficiently salient. Consider the final paragraph of the description:

> So, if these psychologists are right, then once specific earlier events have occurred in a person's life, these events will definitely cause specific later events to occur. For instance, once specific thoughts, desires, and plans occur in the person's mind, they will definitely cause the person to make the specific decision he or she makes. (Nahmias et al. 2007, 224)

The authors focus on perhaps the least threatening aspect of determinism (that our thoughts and desires determine our actions); the description would seem to gloss over the historical aspect of determinism, the notion that these thoughts, desires, and plans are determined by events that occurred before the agents were born.

Nahmias and Murray (2010) have recently conducted a study that more straightforwardly examines the possibility that subjects conflate determinism with fatalism in the Nichols and Knobe study. After giving subjects Nichols and Knobe's description of determinism, they asked them whether the agent's actions could have been different if his or her desires, intentions, and thoughts had been different. The results:

> (i) the vast majority of participants who express *apparent* incompatibilist intuitions interpret determinism to in-

volve bypassing, while those who express *prima facie* compatibilist intuitions tend *not* to, and . . . (ii) there is a dramatic correlation between the degree to which participants take a scenario to involve bypassing and the degree to which they attribute MR and FW to agents in that scenario, but the results also suggest that (iii) the difference in attributions of MR and FW between the abstract conditions is *caused by* people's bypassing interpretations. Subjects may be conflating fatalism with determinism, assuming that agents would perform their actions whether or not they had the intention/desire to do so (207).

I think the general strategy of trying to explain away incompatibilist intuitions is an excellent one. If compatibilists can show that the intuitive force of the TNR principle is based on an error, then we will have good reason to view the intuition as unreliable. Since our commitment to TNR is the primary reason to resist compatibilist accounts of moral responsibility, the case for compatibilism will be all but made. But there is a significant problem with the studies Nahmias and his colleagues appeal to, one that applies to most contemporary experimental work on free will and moral responsibility: Rather than probe for intuitions about the relevant principles philosophers employ in their arguments, the studies probe for intuitions on the compatibility question itself.[11]

The roots of this problem can be seen Nahmias et al.'s seminal article "Is Incompatibilism Intuitive" (2006), the first systematic empirical investigation into our intuitions about free will and determinism. The study probes for intuitions on the compatibility question and finds that the folk give largely compatibilist responses. To explain why such a study is philosophically important, the authors claim (correctly) that arguments for incompatibilism always appeal to intuitions about key premises and cases. Next, they argue (again correctly) that we have no reason to accept incompatibilism unless we find it intuitive upon reflection. The problem arises in the next step of their argument. Nahmias et al. offer a series of quotations from incompatibilists who claim that the folk are natural pretheoretic incompatibilists. One of these incompatibilists, Robert Kane, writes:

> In my experience, most ordinary persons start out as natural incompatibilists. They believe there is some kind of conflict between freedom and determinism; and the idea that freedom and responsibility might be compatible with determinism looks to them at first like a "quagmire of evasion" (William James) or "a wretched subterfuge" (Immanuel Kant). Ordinary persons have to be talked out of this natural incompatibilism by the clever arguments of philosophers. (Kane 1999, 217; quoted in Nahmias et al. 2006, 29)

The authors cite similar passages from Galen Strawson, Thomas Pink, and Laura Ekstrom. The motivation for the studies, then, seems clear. Kane and his fellow incompatibilists are making empirical claims about folk intuitions that can, and should, be tested. Subsequent articles in the experimental literature have followed Nahmias and framed the issue in like manner, selecting from a now-standard menu of passages about the intuitiveness of incompatibilism and then providing data to support or undermine these claims. What is odd from a dialectical standpoint, however, is that the cited passages almost always come from *introductory* sections of incompatibilist articles and books. The role of such passages is, as one might expect, largely rhetorical, to get readers into an incompatibilist mood. There is no incompatibilist *argument* featuring a premise like, say, "free will and moral responsibility are incompatible with determinism" (and for good reason since this would be an obvious case of question-begging). Nor are there arguments of the form (1) we intuitively find free will and moral responsibility to be incompatible with determinism, (2) therefore free will and moral responsibility are incompatible with determinism. So while Nahmias et al. (and the subsequent work that tested intuitions about the compatibility question) are correct in stating that incompatibilist arguments appeal to intuitions, the appeal is for incompatibilist *principles*, not for the compatibility question itself.

What, then, are the implications of the compatibilist results of Nahmias and colleagues? The authors write:

Either determinism obviously precludes free will or those who maintain that it does should offer an explanation as to why it does. The *philosophical* conception of determinism—i.e., that the laws of nature and state of the universe at one time entail the state of the universe at later times—has no obvious conceptual or logical bearing on human freedom and responsibility. So, by claiming that determinism *necessarily* precludes the existence of free will, incompatibilists thereby assume the argumentative burden. (Nahmias et al. 2006, 30)

It seems, however, that incompatibilists can accept that they bear this "argumentative burden" but at the same time claim that they have discharged it—with arguments! After all, Van Inwagen's "consequence argument," Strawson's "basic argument," and Pereboom's "four-case argument," to name only a few, are designed precisely to lead the reader to the conclusion that determinism precludes free will and moral responsibility. Again, the arguments appeal to intuitions, but to intuitions about cases and narrower principles (such as TNR), and not to intuitions about the question posed in the experimental studies. In order to truly test the plausibility of the incompatibilist position, then, we would need to examine the intuitions that support the premises and principles of their arguments and not their introductory rhetoric.

Nahmias and colleagues anticipate an objection of this kind, but their response is problematic. They acknowledge that they have not tested something like the consequence argument directly, but state that their results nonetheless provide *indirect* evidence against its intuitive plausibility, because the scenarios "present conditions in the past that, along with the laws of nature, are sufficient conditions for the agent's action." (2006, 45) They assume, in other words, that philosophically unsophisticated subjects should have somehow internalized or implicitly grasped the consequence argument before ever hearing it! Van Inwagen has received credit for reviving incompatibilism in the past century in large part because he found a non-obvious way of revealing the threat of determinism to free will. Indeed, the whole point of developing an incompatibilist argument (rather than just asserting the conclusion) is to draw out the implications of determinism that might otherwise go unappreciated. It is not clear, then, that the results of these studies give much in the way of indirect evidence against incompatibilist arguments either.

When we apply this criticism to Nahmias et al. (2007) and Nahmias and Murray (2010), we see that the results do not explain away our intuitions about incompatibilist *principles* such as TNR. Rather, at best, they provide an error theory for our intuitions about the compatibility question. Incompatibilists do not, however, rely on *those* intuitions, so they would not need to be too worried if they could be explained away. The independent intuitive plausibility of principles like TNR (e.g., Nagel

1979, Van Inwagen 1983, Strawson 1986) leads me to believe that they cannot be accounted for in the manner that Nahmias and colleagues suspect. Furthermore, the best manipulation and design cases often *emphasize explicitly* that agents' reasoning capacities are part of the causal process leading to behavior—that they are not bypassed—which suggests that the determinism/ fatalism confusion cannot account for our intuitions in these cases.

Finally, it is worth noting that even if the folk are guilty of this confusion, *I* am not guilty of it. The results might show that leaping from determinism to fatalism is tempting and common, so that we should be especially wary of it in our own deliberations about the conditions for moral responsibility. But if we are fully aware of this danger and still find the TNR principle to be intuitive (as I do), then what reason do we have to think that our intuitions are still being corrupted by the confusion?

The Ethical and Pragmatic Benefits of Compatibilism

Thus far, the case for all-things-considered (revisionist) compatibilism is inconclusive. While it is true that we have a strong natural commitment to responsibility related attitudes and practices, many of us seem also to have a natural commitment to a condition for moral responsibility that is incompatible with naturalistic accounts of human agency. There is, moreover, no compelling evidence that the intuitions supporting this condition (and the TNR principle) can be explained away. There may still be ethical and pragmatic considerations, however, that make it reasonable to accept compatibilism over the eliminativist alternative. Indeed, a crucial feature of P. F. Strawson's defense of compatibilism is based on an "assessment of the gains and losses to human life" that the reactive attitudes bring with them. As Bennett puts it: "The greatest single achievement of 'Freedom and Resentment' . . . is its showing how the question 'Ought we to retain praise, blame, etc.?' could be a fundamentally practical one rather than having a strict dependence upon a perpetually troublesome theoretical question" (1980, 30).

So what are the practical benefits of retaining our moral-responsibility practices and attitudes? Strawson and contemporary compatibilists in this tradition (such as Wolf, Watson, and McKenna) focus on the centrality of the reactive attitudes to interpersonal relationships. To regard human beings exclusively with "the objective attitude"—as the eliminativist must—would lead to a cold, bleak, tragic world of human isolation. Embracing compatibilism allows us to retain the natural range of interpersonal attitudes.

In Sommers (2007a), I argue that philosophers have taken an unduly pessimistic view of the objective attitude. They misconstrue what it would mean to deny moral responsibility and renounce the attitudes that presuppose it. I focus on Wolf's (1981) description as it is the clearest and most eloquent expression of the prevailing pessimistic view. Imagining a world in which we regarded each other solely with the objective attitude, Wolf writes:

> We would still imprison murderers and thieves, presumably, and we would still sing praises for acts of courage and charity. We would applaud and criticize, say "thank you" and "for shame" according to whether our neighbors' behavior was or was not to our liking. But these actions and words would have a different, shallower meaning than they have for us now. Our praises would not be expressions of admiration or esteem; our criticisms would not be expressions of indignation or resentment. Rather, they would be bits of positive and negative reinforcement

meted out in the hopes of altering the character of others in ways best suited to our needs. (1981, 391)

The eliminativist can agree with most of the claims in this passage (e.g., "our criticisms would not be expressions of indignation and resentment") but would question the gratuitous use of words like "shallower." Wolf continues:

An act of heroism or of saintly virtue would not inspire us to aim for higher or nobler ideals, nor would it evoke in us a reverence or even admiration for its agent. At best we would think it is a piece of good fortune that people occasionally do perform acts like this. . . . We would not recoil from acts of injustice or cruelty as insults to human dignity, nor be moved by such acts to reflect with sorrow or puzzlement on the tide of events that can bring persons to stoop so low. Rather, we would recognize that the human tendency to perform acts like this is undesirable, a problem to be dealt with, like any other, as scientifically and efficiently as possible. (391)

Here I believe Wolf's worries are mostly groundless. Why, when we take the objective attitude, should an act of heroism not inspire us to aim for this ideal? As noted above in the discussion of Smilansky's illusionism, we do not perform heroic acts merely to deserve praise for them; we perform them because we think the act will serve a worthy purpose. Consider the firemen who entered the World Trade Center on September 11, 2001. Did they risk serious injury and death in order to deserve praise for their bravery? Surely their primary motivation was to save the people trapped inside the building from being burned alive. Such actions inspire admiration and reverence whether or not we attribute any kind of desert-entailing responsibility to the people who performed them. Wolf's second claim is similarly wrong.

Why should we not recoil from acts of cruelty? If Wolf's empha-sis here is on cruelty as an insult to human Dignity with a Kan-tian capital "D," then she is perhaps right. But this does not stop us from recoiling at the sight of cruelty, not as an insult to Dig-nity, but as a cause of intense physical and psychological suffer-ing. We all recoil at the sight of a man being eaten by a tiger, or burned alive, without blaming or resenting the animal or the fire. And of *course* we would be moved to reflect with sorrow at how an event of human cruelty has come to pass. Not blaming the criminal in no way diminishes our sorrow at the suffering of the victim.

Wolf concludes her indictment of the objective attitude with the following observations:

> The most gruesome difference between this world and ours would be reflected in our closest human relation-ships—the relations between siblings, parents and chil-dren, and especially spouses and companions. We would still be able to form some sorts of association that could be described as relationships of friendship and love. One person could find another amusing or useful. One could notice that the presence of a certain person was, like the sound of a favorite song, particularly soothing or invigo-rating. We could choose friends as we now choose cloth-ing or home furnishing or hobbies, according to whether they offer, to a sufficient degree, the proper combination of pleasure and practicality. Attachments of considerable strength can develop on such limited bases. People do, after all, form strong attachments to their cars, their pia-nos, not to mention their pets. Nonetheless I hope it is ob-vious why the words "friendship" and "love" applied to re-lationships in which admiration, respect, and gratitude have no part, might be said to take on a hollow ring. (391)

Once again, the pessimism here seems unmotivated. When we take the objective attitude towards other human beings, we do nothing more than see them as natural things. A human being is still a human being—the most exciting, infuriating, unpredictable, lovable, loathsome natural thing in the world. So we would not *merely* find them useful or amusing. We would not choose our friends like we would choose home furnishings, hobbies, songs, pianos, or pets. We choose friends like we choose human friends—that's all. Nothing in the objective attitude prevents us from recognizing, appreciating, *cherishing* the rich and wonderful qualities of another person. It remains the choice that brings the greatest rewards and the deepest disappointments in all of human existence. Rejecting our responsibility-related attitudes and practices would not change this at all.

The disagreement over these questions is perhaps best seen as an example of how individual differences in temperament can influence our philosophical beliefs. As may be apparent, I have a hard time understanding people who despair at the prospect that we lack free will and moral responsibility. Yet I know that they exist. I know that their feelings are genuine and that they have an equally hard time understanding me. Smilansky (forthcoming) claims to find the optimistic hard determinist perspective "literally incredible." Indeed, he independently uses the example of the 9/11 firemen to argue for the opposite conclusion:

> Think about the firefighters who rushed into the collapsing, burning buildings in 9/11. Envisage a situation in which a few of them who survived, after losing most of their mates, and perhaps being physically harmed themselves, are sitting around and talking about things. Assume that a hard determinist philosopher comes in and tells them that fundamentally they are not better than any common thief or rapist, explaining that ultimately every-

one is what he is, as an inevitable outcome of forces beyond his control. Do you think that they would welcome
this philosopher? Or that, if one or two of them were to
listen to him, and begin to understand and internalize
what he was saying, that those people would not feel that
something very unpleasant and deeply threatening was
being said?

Not only do we both use the same example, but we both litter
our analyses with rhetorical questions—indicating that we
think the answer is obvious! Ultimately, I believe this disagreement boils down to differences in personal psychologies or tem-
peraments. Rational argument can only take us so far. I would
note, however, that Smilansky is wrong to attribute to hard determinists the view that "fundamentally [the firefighters] are
not better than any common thief or rapist." True, hard determinists recognize that we are the inevitable outcome of forces
beyond our control. But these forces still shape us into better or
worse people. Rapists and thieves are bad people. It may not be
their fault that they are bad people, but they are bad people
nonetheless. Similarly, the 9/11 firemen were good people, courageous people, whether or not they deserve credit for their
courage. Only those who are committed to a radically Kantian
understanding of moral worth can claim otherwise.

Nichols's Empirical Defense of Moral Responsibility

Even if one does not despair at the thought of hard determinism, there may be other benefits to holding on to a belief in
moral responsibility. Nichols (2007) offers a pragmatic defense
of responsibility-presupposing attitudes, appealing to evolutionary models and research in experimental economics. (See

chapter 2 for a more detailed description of these theories and models.) Following Frank (1988) and Trivers (1971), Nichols argues that attitudes like moral outrage and guilt help to secure norms that motivate human cooperation. He appeals to the work of Fehr and Gachter (2002) and Boyd et al. (2003), who discuss the role of retributive attitudes in motivating altruistic punishment. Cooperation might deteriorate, Nichols worries, if we were to eliminate the attitudes that are associated with responsibility and desert.

How much support does this research lend to the all-things-considered case for compatibilism? Not very much in my view. Nichols's argument works like this:

1. Reactive attitudes motivate individuals to punish free-riders at a cost.
2. In economic games, when punishment options are re moved, cooperation deteriorates and free-riding behavior increases.
3. Therefore the reactive attitudes are necessary for fostering cooperation.

This argument is not valid, because there may be other ways of raising the expectation of punishment. Indeed, in our society, the law and the criminal justice system exist for this very purpose. The concepts of legal responsibility and legal punishment can be separated from beliefs about *moral* responsibility, as utilitarians since Bentham have repeatedly stressed. The experimental evidence only shows that cooperation suffers when punishment is absent. One might argue that laws are designed to reflect the sentiments and intuitions of society, that without retributive attitudes our laws might not be sufficiently punitive. To this, I reply again that we are considering eliminativism at the level of the individual. As a purely descriptive matter, it is unlikely that most of society will reject responsibility-related beliefs and attitudes. The function of moral anger only requires that potential offenders *expect* to find it in others as a response to wrongdoing. Any particular individual, then, can reject attitudes like moral anger without undermining its function—as long as he or she stays in the relative minority.

Indeed, Nichols himself notes that the best strategy for an individual in public goods games is never to punish, as long as there are enough punishers in the population to sustain cooperation. But he accuses anti-retributivists of "second-order free-riding" since they get the benefits of retributivism without paying the costs (Nichols 2007, 426, n. 11). In one sense he is correct. Presumably, however, eliminativists who engage in this kind of free-riding do so not for personal gain, but rather because of their commitment to a principle of fairness (the TNR principle). Surely the pragmatic gains of a position adopted for moral reasons should not count *against* the position.

CONCLUSION

The goal of this chapter has been to outline arguments for versions of libertarianism and compatibilism that are consistent with the broader metaskeptical thesis. I considered the "all-things-considered" cases for both compatibilism and libertarianism for members of my "intuition group"—people with starting intuitions and attitudes about responsibility that resemble my own. I argued that libertarianism is an implausible alternative because its epistemic costs outweigh its alleged pragmatic and moral benefits. The more promising case for compatibilism, I argued, relies on questionable assumptions. I will continue to challenge those assumptions in the final chapter as I develop the case for eliminativism about moral responsibility.

CHAPTER SEVEN

A Very Tentative Metaskeptical Endorsement of Eliminativism about Moral Responsibility

Thomas Nagel captures the intuitive appeal of eliminativism about responsibility perfectly when he writes:

> Something in the idea of agency is incompatible with actions being events, and people being things. But as the external determinants of what someone has done are gradually exposed, in their effect on consequences, character, and choice itself, it becomes gradually clear that actions are events and people things. Eventually nothing remains that can be ascribed to a responsible self, and we are left with nothing but a portion of the larger sequence of events, which can be deplored or celebrated, but not blamed or praised.[1]

As a philosophical naturalist, I accept that actions are events and that people are things—wondrous complex things, but things nonetheless. The objective attitude (as Strawson calls it), in which actions are deplored or celebrated but not blamed or praised, seems an appropriate attitude to adopt towards natural things. Consequently, for many years I believed that denying moral responsibility was the only intellectually respectable view to adopt.

But things are not so simple for the metaskeptic. When I confidently endorsed first-order skepticism, I believed that the question "what would happen if we rejected moral responsibility" was completely independent of the question of whether we *were* morally responsible.[2] One implication of metaskepticism is that we must see the two questions as connected. Moral responsibility is not a mind-independent property like "transparent" that can be assigned objectively or universally when certain conditions are met. The answer to the question of whether we can be morally responsible boils down to a subjective all-things-considered judgment that takes many factors into account, including the ethical and practical consequences of each alternative. Chapter 6 concluded with an assessment of the pragmatic benefits of the compatibilist position. I will begin this chapter by examining the moral and practical implications of denying moral responsibility and adopting the objective attitude on an exclusive basis. Next, I will consider arguments that attempt to explain away or debunk the intuition that people can be morally responsible for their behavior. Finally, I will discuss an important concession to compatibilism, one that prevents me from arriving at a more confident endorsement of the eliminativist conclusion.

CAN WE DENY MORAL RESPONSIBILITY AND LEAD RICH AND FULFILLING LIVES?

Everyone concedes that we adopt the objective attitude towards other human beings on occasion. As Strawson (2003) notes, we take this attitude towards small children, schizophrenics, and even, every so often, towards the "mature and normal" as a refuge from "the strains of involvement." What libertarians and compatibilists in the Strawsonian tradition worry about are the implications of *exclusively* regarding people with the objective eye. By shifting in and back out of the objective perspective we are able to retain the natural range of interpersonal attitudes, as well as our intuitive beliefs about moral responsibility. Strawson claims in addition that the objective attitude leads us to see people as "objects of social policy" and the person as "the subject of . . . treatment" (2003, 79). According to Strawson, we are unable to quarrel or reason with someone we view from the objective perspective. We can "at most pretend to quarrel, or reason, with him" (79). As far as I can tell, Strawson provides little or no argument to back these claims, so I will withhold judgment about them for now. The central question is whether we can retain the attitudes and values that we cherish as human beings if we no longer regard ourselves and others as morally responsible agents. If compatibilists and libertarians are right that rejecting moral responsibility and adopting the objective attitude fulltime would lead to a cold, bleak, "practically inconceivable" "tragic world of human isolation," this would considerably undermine the case for eliminativism about moral responsibility. Proponents of this position, then, owe an account of how human life could retain its richness, value, and fulfillment in a world without morally responsible agents. In what follows, I will try to sketch the outlines of such an account. [3]

Sally the Nihilist

Imagine a person, Sally, who is convinced by incompatibilist arguments, the TNR principle, and the injustice of blaming and punishing people for acts that are ultimately beyond their control.[4] She resolves, upon deliberation, to adopt the objective attitude, to regard actions as events and people as things. She becomes a nihilist about moral responsibility (though not necessarily about objective moral values in general). What will her interpersonal relationships look like? Which of our interpersonal and self-regarding attitudes are consistent with her nihilism and which are not? Let's consider them one by one.

RESENTMENT AND INDIGNATION

Resentment is the paradigm of a responsibility-presupposing attitude. We feel resentment when we believe that people have wronged us and deserve blame for doing so. We only resent human beings because only human beings, we imagine, have the kind of freedom that makes this attitude appropriate. We do not resent a dog for tracking mud into the house, or a computer for crashing, or the weather for ruining graduation—or if we do resent these things in the heat of the moment, upon reflection, we consider the attitude to be inappropriate. According to P. F. Strawson, the closely related feeling of indignation arises when we vicariously experience another's wrong and, again, believe that the perpetrator is morally responsible for the wrongdoing. We resent injuries inflicted on us; we are indignant at the injuries of others.

To Sally, resentment makes no sense. We do not resent a tree that falls down and destroys our house; so we should not resent a thief who breaks in and steals everything in that house. Both events are part of the natural causal structure of the universe. We may be angry, furious in fact, about the theft; we may be deeply sorrowful (if, say, among the items lost were old honeymoon photographs and scrapbooks). But not resentful. As Sally looks at the robbery, she thinks that the thief could have refrained from robbing the house only in the sense that the tree could have refrained from falling.

Would ridding ourselves of resentment be such a great loss? Resentment is a negative emotion that eats away at us when we feel we have been wronged or taken advantage of. It is often triggered by minor offenses—being cut off on the highway, a slight at work, a critic's snide remark in the *New York Review of Books*. Ridding ourselves of resentment in such cases would likely improve our lives, make us more easygoing, less consumed with bitterness. A person who takes a nihilist's view of moral responsibility has a reason to resist these feelings. Rather than relentlessly judging the actions of her friends and acquaintances, Sally may try to appreciate them in all of their complexity. She may attempt to take what Nussbaum (1993) calls the "novelistic approach," where judgment takes a back seat to understanding and compassion.

Of course, the more horrible the offense, the harder this will be to do. If someone harms a member of Sally's family, her resentment will likely boil over. She may have an uncontrollable desire for vengeance. Perhaps she *should* have an uncontrollable desire for vengeance. (I will return to this point below). But even feelings this strong can diminish, succeeded by a lasting grief. And grief, no matter how passionate or intense, is perfectly consistent with the objective attitude and the denial of moral responsibility.

GRATITUDE

Gratitude is a complicated feeling for Sally, because it has a number of aspects. There seems to be an aspect of gratitude that presupposes that the object of the gratitude deserves praise for his or her actions. But there is also an aspect of gratitude that does not presuppose this. We are often grateful for a cool breeze, or a magnificent view. By contrast, we are not resentful of a hot muggy day or a minus 50-degree wind-chill. (And I speak from experience, having lived most recently in Morris, Minnesota and Houston, Texas.) So Sally must ask herself how she is to distinguish these two components of gratitude when it comes to human actions.

Suppose Sally, after visiting an ATM, drops her wallet on the street, and later a woman picks it up. She looks at the address on the license and drives out to Sally's house to return it. How should Sally react to this act of good will? Someone like Wolf or Smilansky might say that Sally should just take the wallet, thank the woman (for that will reinforce the behavior, making it more likely that she will repeat the action in the future), and close the door, her true manner cold and indifferent to the woman. After all, this woman does not *deserve praise* for her act. It was just a natural event. The woman is not *responsible* for being the kind of person who goes out of her way to commit a kind and thoughtful act, and so there is nothing to be grateful for.

As with the Wolf passages discussed in chapter 6, the description here is factually accurate but unnecessarily bleak. Sally should thank the woman, but not only because it may reinforce the behavior. She should also thank her because she deeply appreciates the gesture. And while it is true that the woman does not ultimately deserve praise for her actions (ultimately, Sally believes, it is a matter of luck that she became the kind of person who performs them), there is no reason for Sally to be cold-hearted toward her. She can warmly appreciate the gesture and the person who performed it without attributing desert-entailing responsibility to her. Sally can *exult* in the gesture if she wants; she can think, "What a nice world it is that produces clumsy, absentminded people like me who drop money-stuffed wallets, and sweet, unselfish women like her who return them." True, much of this appreciation does not pertain to the woman herself, but instead to the world that produced her. Nevertheless it is *her*, the woman, that Sally is celebrating. And the greater the heroes, the more profound our feelings of appreciation will be. It is true that we are not attributing to these heroes dignity and respect as autonomous agents. But this does not prevent us from admiring and applauding their characters and the actions that arise from their characters. We are grateful to the world for having such people in it, and we appreciate the heroes themselves for being what they are (even if they are not morally responsible for what they are). This is a deep, warm, *un*bleak, *un*barren, *un*ironic appreciation, and it is entirely consistent with denying moral responsibility.

Forgiveness, like gratitude, has multiple aspects. For Sally, there is certainly a sense in which *tout comprendre c'est tout pardonner* is true. If no one is morally responsible for any act, however heinous, then everyone should ultimately be forgiven. Nietzsche's description of Mirabeau is relevant here:

> Mirabeau had no memory for insults and vile actions done him and was unable to forgive simply because he— forgot. . . . Such a man shakes off with a *single* shrug many vermin that eat deep into others; here alone genuine "love of one's enemies" is possible—supposing it to be possible at all on earth. (1992, 475)

But there is another sense of forgiveness that survives. It requires that we follow Richard Double's (1991) advice and replace the question, "Was S morally responsible for *a*?" with "Was *a* reflective of S's character?" (228). Often when we forgive someone for an action, we believe that the act was not an essential and ineradicable part of his or her character. There are a lot of determining factors at work when it comes to how people act, many of which are unrelated to the type of human being that the agent essentially is. If someone betrays Sally but she believes that the act was "out of character," she may forgive him. Why? Because she believes that the act does not reflect how the person truly is. Her decision about whether or not to forgive him will then depend on whether she believes his regret is sincere and whether he is capable (in the compatibilist sense) of refraining from committing the types of action that make her unhappy.[5] One might object here that by Sally's lights, he does not deserve blame whether or not it reflects his character. Aren't her criteria of forgiveness arbitrary and unfair? No. It is true that people with truly bad characters should ultimately be forgiven, but this does not mean that Sally wants to hang out with them. A bad person is still a bad person. It is not their fault that they are bad people, but all the same Sally wants to avoid them when she can.

LOVE

Love is the emotion many philosophers find to be most endangered by the objective attitude and the absence of free will and moral responsibility. Laura Ekstrom, for example, writes:

> Concerning at least certain of our personal relationships, crucial to our sense that they are genuine is the assumption that the participants are free in adopting whatever emotional stances they take, including their commitment, or lack of it, to each other. To suppose that human beings are wholly without free will seems naturally to require that we give up some of the satisfaction we derive from our relationships, since a view of persons who act, but never freely, entails that our speech, thoughts, emotions, and body motions, never count as free expressions of ourselves. One type of relationship especially illustrative of

this dependence of a sense of genuineness upon an assumption of free will is the romantic sort of personal relationship. (2000, 16)

Here Ekstrom echoes P. F. Strawson (2003, 79), who writes that the objective attitude cannot include "the sort of love which adults can sometimes be said to feel reciprocally for each other;" and Wolf (1981, 391) who "hopes it is obvious why the words 'friendship' and 'love' would take on a hollow ring under the objective attitude."

This is certainly the majority view, and it is often accepted as obvious. But as Pereboom notes, "the thesis that love between mature persons would be subverted if hard incompatibilism were true requires more thorough argument than Strawson has provided" (2001, 202). And not just Strawson. No theorist that I know of has provided any rigorous argument showing that denying moral responsibility would endanger even the most tragic, passionate, romantic, or blissful kinds of love that exist. The conclusion is simply assumed, and then underscored with gloomy metaphors. Ekstrom cites with approval the remarks of philosopher W. S. Anglin who writes that "it is an essential part of our most intimate relationships that we view our love as a 'freely given gift.' If I learn that my spouse loves me only because this 'love' is the inevitable product of some childhood experience then the whole relationship takes on a strange and dark color" (2000, 12).

Sally, by contrast, cannot see why love must be viewed as a "freely given gift." It would be disturbing, she supposes, if some active conscious agent had hypnotized her husband into loving her. But her nihilism presumes no such thing. It presumes only that the person who loves is not the ultimate source of his or her feelings and action. Of course childhood and adult experiences, in conjunction with heredity, have resulted in the love that husbands and wives feel for one another. But why on earth would that undermine the genuineness of the feeling itself?

Ekstrom and Anglin are libertarians, of course; compatibilists will agree that inevitable or determined love can be genuine. The issue that divides Strawsonian compatibilists and nihilists is whether we need to see our loved ones as responsible in the compatibilist sense. But like the issue of objective worth (see chapter 6), I do not see the connection between love and any type of moral responsibility, compatibilist or libertarian. Many of the world's most passionate love stories—think Wagner's *Tristan and Isolde*—involve a love that was generated by fate, potions, or arrows. Consider too the relationship many of us have with our pets. Those of us who love our dogs and believe the love to be reciprocated form this deep bond without presuming anything about moral responsibility and certainly without in any way viewing the love of a dog as a freely given gift. We know that it is a result of our having cared for them, played with them, walked them, and fed them since they were puppies. Moreover, we know that dogs have been bred to form deep attachments with human beings—their loyalty and eagerness to please have been both artificially and naturally selected for. We know that they do not reflectively endorse their feelings of love, or subject them to the light of reason. We know this, and we don't care. We still love them, and we view their love for us as genuine.

Objection: But that's love for a dog! How can you possibly compare it with the love of two rational mature adults? Response: the two kinds of love *are* different, but this difference has nothing to do with moral responsibility. The difference is that human beings have far more complex, maddening, and exciting ways of expressing and feeling love for one another. In saying that both human beings and dogs are not free and morally responsible agents, we are not saying that human beings are just like dogs. Both dogs and humans have two eyes, but that does not mean that my love for dogs is identical to my love for humans. A human being is a human being. We must always keep this simple tautology in mind whenever someone wishes to dismiss the emotions of a responsibility nihilist as deficient. The love we feel for our husbands, wives, partners, close friends, and children is deeper in many ways than the love we feel for our dogs, just as our love for dogs is deeper than our love for a good wine. Romantic love, friendships, parent-child relationships evolve because of who we are, how we naturally complement each other, the good times, good jokes, and tragedies that we go through together. None of this is undermined by the objective attitude. None of this requires a belief in desert-entailing moral responsibility.[6]

Of course, some will not be persuaded by this defense of "unfree love." They have conceived of and defined genuine love or friendship as essentially involving a deep form of free will and moral responsibility. Again, Smilansky's views serve as a useful contrast. He writes:

> But with all of the years I've spent on the free will problem, and although I am convinced that [libertarian free will] is nonsense, I can still feel the loss, and want to fool myself. Do I want my daughter to feel that *I* had real choices? Would it *matter* to me if she saw my efforts on her behalf as, well, just the way I was built, as ultimately beyond my control? Of course! (Smilansky, forthcoming, 19)

Once again, I am struck by how differences in individual temperament affect this debate. If I had posed those very same questions, I would answer just as emphatically, "Of course not!"

It makes absolutely no difference to me whether my daughter sees my choices and efforts on her behalf as beyond my control. I know my attachment to her is due in part to kin selection and cultural forces. Even if Eliza were not the smartest, sweetest, funniest, most beautiful six-year-old on the planet, I would probably love her as much as I do now. To me, the depth of feeling, the appreciation, the joy of being around one another, is enough when it comes to love.

SELF-REACTIVE ATTITUDES: GUILT, REGRET, AND PRIDE

We now have a better sense of how Sally might view others if she were to live in a manner that is consistent with denying moral responsibility But how might she view herself? The "self-reactive" attitudes that would seem to be most affected are guilt, regret, and pride.

On the face of it, denying moral responsibility seems to undermine guilt, in the same way that it undermines resentment. After all, if others do not deserve blame for their actions, neither do we. And if we are not blameworthy for our regrettable actions, why should we feel guilty?

It is important first to recognize that one aspect of guilt *is* truly inconsistent with the objective attitude. This is the aspect that presumes that we are blameworthy for our behavior, a notion that Sally would find irrational. But there is also an important difference between our own behavior and the behavior of others. We have what Bruce Waller has called *take-charge responsibility* (TCR) for our own actions. (1998, 40). We can deliberate, make plans, and guide our future conduct. We do not have TCR for the actions of others. The feeling (or self-reactive attitude) of guilt is deeply intertwined with this TCR. Guilt is a signal to us that our actions are regrettable. It informs us that it would have been better if we had not performed them. It's also a signal that we should make reparations. Since we have some compatibilist—or "take charge"—control over our actions in the future, we can allow our feelings of guilt and regret to guide us. We can note that the action caused us to have these negative feelings, that it caused suffering to others, and then we can resolve not to perform similar actions in the future.

The aspect of guilt that does *not* fit with the objective attitude is the kind of morbid hand wringing that keeps us awake all night thinking about what might have been. When we feel this aspect of guilt, we dwell on the action, we analyze it, replaying the situation over and over in our head, thinking about all the different ways we *should* have responded. We do this not with an eye to future improvement, but with basic sadness and humiliation about the way we behaved. Again, it is tricky to call this aspect inconsistent with the objective attitude because it is bound up with the first aspect. If denying moral responsibility mitigates the negative aspect of guilt, will the motivation to avoid similar behavior in the future remain as strong? Will we be as motivated to make reparations? Maybe, maybe not. Certainly, we can still *recognize* the negative effects of our actions without blaming ourselves for it. The objective attitude may allow Sally to get a little more sleep, thinking "what's done is done, let's just apologize and not do it again."

The same reasoning applies to pride. There is an aspect of pride that presupposes that we deserve praise for our accomplishments. But there are aspects of pride that do not. When we do a nice turn for someone, or write a good essay, or perform well at work, a feeling of fulfillment accompanies these actions. There is absolutely no reason to deny this feeling, or to try to train ourselves out of having it. It exists, it is natural. (Recall the pride that Joe took in his natural ability to make people laugh.) This aspect of pride truly is non-propositional—it does not assume anything about our own praiseworthiness. Just as a beautiful woman looks admiringly at herself in the mirror, Sally may appreciate the kind of person she has become. She may admire certain qualities—loyalty to her friends, a desire to help others, the creativity she displays in her art, the dedication she shows to her work. Cleopatra presumably did not feel she was responsible for the beauty of her nose, but she certainly took pride in its length and elegance.

What *is* inconsistent with the objective attitude is the hint of self-righteousness that sometimes accompanies such self-appreciation—the thought "why can't other people be as good as I am?" Recognizing that all the people whom we love, respect, and cherish are not responsible for being who they are may help to lessen the disdain and contempt we sometimes feel for those who are not fortunate enough to make it into this charmed circle. But the self-appreciation itself, as long as it does not involve a belief in desert-entailing responsibility, is something Sally can consistently embrace.

THE FRINGE BENEFITS OF NIHILISM

Finally, how might Sally view the world of public affairs now that she denies moral responsibility? This is an area where the upside of nihilism about moral responsibility becomes quite readily apparent. Reading newspapers or blogs, talking to friends, coworkers, colleagues, watching television news, listening to talk radio, it often seems as though we live in a state of perpetual moral outrage. Sally will find this kind of indignation irrational. It does not matter if you are a conservative outraged at the prospect of gay marriage, or a liberal outraged by the banning of it, the resentment and bitterness we feel towards our opponents makes little sense. Sally will likely retain the disposition to become indignant—it is a powerful psychological drive. But she will also work to soften its impact on her psyche. When she notices the high-pitched semi-whine of moral indignation creeping into her voice, she will take a deep breath and stop. Although she is an anti-war liberal she will realize that Dick Cheney no more deserves blame for bringing us to war under false pretenses than Barack Obama deserves praise for opposing the war. Taking the objective attitude will still of course allow her to vote for and finance candidates whose policies she favors. But there will be no hatred, no resentment for candidates who oppose those policies. A liberal nihilist would believe that it is simply a matter of bad luck that Sean Hannity is the type of person he is. And the conservative would believe the same about Michael Moore. Once we reflect that *all people*, including those who hold abhorrent political views, are not responsible for being who they are, we can rid ourselves of the high toned self-righteousness that poisons most political discussions. And then we can work productively to convince people that our own views are more credible. Will we be successful at banishing soul-rotting anger and indignation at all times? Of course not. But over time, Sally can acquire a view of life that is compassionate, pragmatic, cheerful, and that (as Einstein has written) gives humor its due. It is the view of life that scientific naturalists take to the field and novelists take to the world they wish to portray. The goal is to learn, appreciate, describe. Moral posturing is left to the politicians.

SUMMING UP

The goal of this section has been to show that one can deny moral responsibility and live a rich and fulfilling life. I have argued that the negative ethical implications of this position are considerably exaggerated and that it can plausibly result in a life with less resentment, bitterness, self-righteousness, and remorse. There are no overwhelming ethical or practical reasons to embrace a positive conception of moral responsibility. Consequently, for those who have a strong commitment to TNR as a basic principle of fairness, eliminativism may be an attractive alternative to revisionist compatibilism.

CAN WE EXPLAIN AWAY THE PMR BELIEF?

In chapter 6, I examined a recent attempt by Nahmias and colleagues to explain away incompatibilist intuitions. Many first-order skeptics or nihilists about moral responsibility (my earlier self included) have also been tempted by debunking strategies. The nihilist goal is to explain away what I have called PMR, our persistent belief that people can be morally responsible for their behavior. In Sommers (2005) and (2007b), for example, I argued that the PMR belief is adaptive, and that we would therefore have adopted it whether or not it reflected the truth about moral responsibility. I concluded that since we now have sound independent arguments against moral responsibility, we should excise our belief in moral responsibility with a confident slice of Occam's razor.

I no longer think that this is a viable strategy. The first problem is that the explanation for our commitment to moral responsibility assumes too great a uniformity in the environmental challenges our ancestors faced. As I argued in Part One, different responsibility norms are better suited to different environments. One might raise "genetic-fallacy" worries about the argument as well. Even if my account of the evolution of responsibility beliefs were accurate, it would not be valid to infer that the beliefs were false or even undermined. But of course the argument is not meant to work on its own but rather in conjunction with strong independent arguments against moral responsibility. (The same is true for evolutionary arguments against objective moral values in general; e.g., Joyce [2001, 2006] and Ruse [1986].) The role of an evolutionary account is only to provide an explanation for why we might have beliefs that do not reflect underlying reality. At most, it tries to undermine realism as the default position and shift the burden of proof to the realist.

The real problem with the argument is not that it commits the genetic fallacy but rather that it does not consider whether the truth of our beliefs about the conditions of moral responsibility is in part *constituted by* our attitudes, practices, and norms. When attempting to debunk beliefs about witchcraft or psychic powers, it is sufficient to provide a plausible naturalistic explanation of the observed phenomena. If moral responsibility were conceived of as an objective property or capacity (like having psychic powers), then the argument could provide a valuable explaining away of our beliefs in these properties. But if we have a more naturalistic or constructivist understanding of moral responsibility, then the debunking strategy goes awry. An evolutionary explanation for why fatty foods taste delicious does not explain away the deliciousness of bacon. The truth of "bacon is delicious" is constituted by how bacon tastes to us. Since the approach outlined in chapter 5 for arriving at all-things-considered responsibility judgments is a constructivist one, debunking strategies that rely on Occam's razor do not seem applicable. There is nothing metaphysically exotic or queer about weighing intuitions and coming to all-things-considered judgments.

But there may be other viable debunking strategies. One can try to show that certain intuitions—even considered intuitions—are grounded in demonstrably false beliefs. Recall that this was the strategy adopted by Nahmias et al. when they argued that the intuitive force of incompatibilism is rooted in our mistake of confusing determinism with fatalism (the view that our desires and intentions have no effect on what will happen to us). Similarly, one might try to show that the considered intuitions that ground a belief in moral responsibility arise from erroneous understandings of human behavior. Greene and Cohen (2004) and Ross and Shestowsky (2003) develop a critique of moral responsibility along these lines, arguing that our responsibility judgments are grounded in false beliefs about human autonomy. According to Greene and Cohen, our judgments reflect the presupposition of a dualist agent-self, which allows us to attribute responsibility to others while retaining our incompatibilist intuitions. Ross and Shestowsky appeal to the situationist literature in social psychology, claiming that our responsibility attributions are contaminated by a "dispositional bias" that overrates the influence of stable character traits and underestimates the power of situational factors to govern behavior. Both authors conclude that since our current responsibility judgments are based on empirically false beliefs, we should reject the notion of desert—at least when it comes to issuing punishments.

One might wonder if we are capable of overcoming these biases and beliefs given how deeply rooted they are in our psychologies. Greene and Cohen offer the following instructive analogy in their argument:

> Modern physics tells us that space is curved. Nevertheless, it may be impossible for us to see the world as anything other than flatly Euclidean in our day-to-day lives. And there are, no doubt, deep evolutionary explanations for our Euclidean tendencies. Does it then follow that we are forever bound by our innate Euclidean psychology? The answer depends on the domain of life in question. In navi-

gating the aisles of the grocery store, an intuitive, Euclidean representation of space is not only adequate, but probably inevitable. However, when we are, for example,
planning the launch of a spacecraft, we can and should
make use of relativistic physical principles that are less intuitive but more accurate. In other words, a Euclidean perspective is not necessary for all practical purposes, and the
same may be true for our implicit commitment to free will
and retributivism. For most day-to-day purposes it may be
pointless or impossible to view ourselves or others in this
detached sort of way. But—and this is the crucial point—it
may not be pointless or impossible to adopt this perspective when one is deciding what the criminal law should be
or whether a given defendant should be put to death for
his crimes. These may be special situations, analogous to
those routinely encountered by "rocket scientists," *in
which the counter-intuitive truth* that we legitimately ignore most of the time can and should be acknowledged.
(Greene and Cohen 2004, 1784, my italics)

Greene and Cohen refer here to desert in the context of criminal law, but the analogy may apply in the broader context of
desert assignments as well. The basic idea is this: it is psychologically difficult for human beings to accept that no one is morally responsible for their behavior, and in many contexts we may
not have to. At the same time, just as relativist principles reflect
the truth about space, responsibility nihilism reflects the *truth*
about desert. When the stakes are high—in establishing the
principles of criminal justice, for example—we are obligated to
acknowledge this truth.[7]

   If the authors are correct that responsibility intuitions and
judgments are rooted in biases and false beliefs, then we clearly

need to take this into account when forming new all-things-considered judgments. But we cannot yet infer that the rational response is to reject our assignments of desert. The empirical nature of physics makes Greene and Cohen's analogy slightly misleading. We judge the truth or plausibility of a particular theory in physics by its degree of predictive success and explanatory power. When we launch rockets into space, for example, we accept relativistic principles precisely because of their value in predicting the behavior of the rockets. There is no such straightforward way of evaluating responsibility assignments. Theories denying responsibility do not make successful predictions. Hard incompatibilism is a theory about the *injustice* of holding people morally responsible for acts that are caused by factors beyond their control. Empirical inquiry can tell us whether or not we have a particular capacity or type of control—but it cannot tell us whether it is fair or appropriate to blame or praise people with whatever capacities and control they have.

Greene and Cohen may argue that we are intuitive incompatibilists and therefore only assign moral responsibility because of our empirically false belief in libertarian free will. Perhaps future experimental work will bear this out. But even if we begin as intuitive incompatibilists who operate under the misconception that we are dualist agent-selves, we might nevertheless revise our understanding of the conditions of moral responsibility in light of information about the real causes of human behavior (Vargas 2004, Nichols 2007).

The following analogy can illustrate this point. There are some people, call them "romantics," who conceive of love as something that is entirely selfless and not subject to naturalistic explanation. Romantics believe that love for one's children or partners must have its source in something other than neurophysiology and the struggle for survival and reproduction. *Real* love in their conception involves a meeting of two kindred souls or an intertwining of spirits (or choose your favorite non-naturalistic account of love). For Romantics, love is not love if it is the result of neurons firing because it was adaptive for our ancestors that those neurons fire. Now imagine that the romantics learn about the proximate and ultimate mechanisms governing our feelings of love. They become convinced that naturalistic evolutionary accounts can fully explain the experience they once attributed to a meeting of two kindred souls. Romantics will undoubtedly find this new way of viewing love discouraging and depressing. Initially, they may begin to doubt that they *truly* love their children, friends, and partners. But would these naturalistic accounts debunk their belief that they love their children or partners? Not necessarily. True, it sounds strange to the Romantic ear to claim that real love can have a mechanistic foundation. But it sounds just as strange to claim that they do not love their children. They adore their children, they are devoted to them, would kill anyone who tried to harm them. As a Romantic, it arguably makes more sense to take the revisionist route rather than the eliminativist one, to substantially revise their concept of love rather than to deny its existence.

The existence of love, then, seems resistant to general debunking strategies.[8] We might debunk a particular belief—that Susan loves Doug, for example (by showing that the belief is a result of brainwashing perhaps)—but it is hard to imagine an explanation that would show that all beliefs about love are false. Strawson, of course, makes the same claim about moral responsibility. He argues that we can question whether a particular person is an appropriate target of blame and resentment, but that we cannot deny moral responsibility as a general principle. The framework of responsibility-related attitudes and beliefs re-

sists such an "external" critique. If beliefs about love and responsibility are analogous in the appropriate way, Strawson's argument gains strong support.

It is worth examining how the concepts of moral responsibility and love map on to one another in this analogy. Romantics
believe that the nature of true love is not compatible with mechanistic accounts of human feeling. Incompatibilists believe that
the nature of desert-entailing responsibility is not compatible
with naturalistic or deterministic accounts of human agency.
When Romantics learn about the true basis for love, they conclude, upon reflection, that they should revise rather than eliminate their concept of love. Should incompatibilists about responsibility do the same?

Before the compatibilist or revisionist becomes overconfident, let us consider a contrasting case. Imagine a group called
the Exorcists who believe in demonic possession. When people
behave in extremely unusual and unpredictable ways, Exorcists
call them "possessed." The possession helps to explain their behavior. Built into the concept of possession for Exorcists is the
existence of a demon or supernatural being who does the possessing. Now imagine that the Exorcists learn about diseases
like epilepsy and various other medical disorders. They also
read theories from cognitive science about agency detection—
the human predilection to attribute unexplained events to some
kind of causal agency. The theories seem to account for their
impulse to attribute abnormal behavior to a demon or possessing force. At this point, they have two options. They can either
revise the concept of possession to incorporate this new information, or they can reject the concept as not picking out anything in the world. Here eliminativism rather than revision
seems to be the most reasonable option. The idea of a demon or
higher agency is too essential for the concept of possession.

When we reject the existence of a higher agency, the concept of possession is no longer useful, except perhaps as a metaphor. Naturalistic accounts have in this case explained away or debunked widespread beliefs in demonic possession. Moreover, even if a large part of the general public were unaware of the naturalistic accounts and continued to find it intuitive that people are possessed, we would no longer want to base policy decisions on these widespread intuitions. No one should suffer because of the general public's ignorance about the causes of abnormal behavior.

So then, is the concept of moral responsibility more like love or more like demonic possession? This is a difficult question, and there do not seem to be determinate criteria for providing an answer. Part of the answer, however, surely depends on how essential the notion of libertarian free will is to the concept of moral responsibility. The feelings associated with love—devotion, adoration, protectiveness etc.—are, in my view, enough to constitute the concept of love, even after non-natural associations are rejected. By contrast, when one rejects the notion of a possessing agent, the belief "Damien is possessed" is stripped of an essential feature. Perhaps not surprisingly, the question of how essential the notion of libertarian free will is to moral responsibility will depend on how intuitive we find the TNR principle to be.

Another factor to consider is the centrality of the concept to our moral and non-moral lives. Beliefs about love play a large role in explaining human behavior and character. If I take the belief "I love my daughter" or "I love my wife" to be false, then what could account for my attitudes and behavior towards them? Beliefs about possession are less central to life, even in superstitious cultures—since instances of alleged possession are rare. Where does the function of the moral responsibility concept lie along this spectrum? It seems that in order to evaluate the success of debunking strategies in the moral responsibility debate we have to look to the very factors we have already been considering in the wide reflective equilibrium process.

An Important Concession to the Compatibilist

As I have mentioned, my dissertation defended an optimistic denial of moral responsibility, the position Smilansky calls "happy hard determinism." I thought the arguments against moral responsibility were unshakable and that accepting the truth of the skeptical conclusion would have significant benefits for human lives. It was during this period that my daughter Eliza was born, and this event triggered a nagging doubt in my mind that I have not resolved to this day. I (almost instantly) imagined a scenario in which someone deliberately and willfully harmed her. This person met all the normal compatibilist conditions, but not the incompatibilist conditions that I believed were necessary for true blameworthiness. I told my class at the time that if this were to occur, God forbid, I would feel that the offender deserved to suffer for the act— I would feel this more strongly than just about anything else. (I would probably want to dish out some of this suffering myself.) It would be obscene, I thought, to worry about whether the person was *causa sui*, ultimately responsible for his character, or whether factors that trace back beyond his control led him to perform this act. If someone said to me, "But what about the TNR principle?" I would respond, "Screw the TNR Principle!"[9]

More importantly, even at the time, when I was just imagining this scenario, I believed this to be the *right or appropriate* response. It would be wrong *not* to feel this way. In other words, I endorsed this retributive response upon reflection. However, I did not feel that this retributive response was appropriate for offenders who did not meet certain basic compatibilist conditions. A person who was completely crazy, or who was manipulated into performing the act, should not, I thought, be held morally responsible. I would likely feel retributive anyway, but upon reflection that response would seem irrational.

The issue here is not that my incompatibilist intuitions had weakened. I found the four-case argument and the basic argument no less compelling, and the TNR principle just as intuitively plausible. And I had no doubt that my retributive attitudes were rooted in my evolutionary and cultural history. But this knowledge did not undermine my basic stance. I still believed it would be deeply inappropriate to favor incompatibilist intuitions over my intuition that the guy who harmed my daughter deserved to suffer for that crime. When asked why the same reasoning should not apply to other people's daughters (and relatives and friends), I did not have a good answer.

The challenge then, is this. Since intuitions are the ultimate arbiters for theories of responsibility, and in this case, upon reflection, the force of my retributive intuition is greater than the incompatibilist (TNR) intuition, it seems I should rethink my all-things-considered rejection of compatibilism.

Incompatibilists may object that I am conflating psychological responses and normative judgments concerning the imagined offense. As Thomas Nadelhoffer has put it, "Why not just say that under certain tragic circumstances, even you could be induced to have retributivist intuitions of such force that they would effectively undermine your ability to think clearly about the issues at hand?"[10] But in what sense was I thinking unclearly? It is true that retributive feelings are rooted in a specific evolutionary and cultural history, and so we should not assume that they point to some mind-independent normative fact about the appropriateness of desert. But the same is true of our incompatibilist commitments and intuitions. As a metaskeptic, I do not believe that there are mind-independent normative facts about desert beyond my own all-things-considered judgments. There is no straightforward way for evolutionary explanations to debunk our beliefs about the conditions for moral responsibility. If we are aware of the origins of the intuitions and take the origins into account when formulating considered judgments, how is our thinking unclear? How is the judgment rooted in error?

There may be a more indirect way to explain away my retributive feelings in this case, however. Tom Clark notes, "Perhaps you feel that it's 'obscene' and 'deeply inappropriate' to give any weight to incompatibilist intuitions because you think that being swayed by them would show (to yourself or others) that you don't *really* love your daughter."[11] This is a promising line of argument. My commitment to the TNR principle, strong as it is, is weaker than my conviction that I love daughter. So if I thought that accepting the TNR principle (and denying the responsibility of the criminal) meant implicitly that I did not sufficiently love my daughter, I would say farewell to the TNR principle. But as Clark notes, there is in fact no connection between how much we love our family members and a reflective judgment about the blameworthiness of someone who harms them. So if Clark's hypothesis is correct, then my considered intuition in favor of compatibilism would be based on a false belief and in that sense explained away.

But this strategy runs into some difficulties as well. Recall that my response differs when the offender does not meet certain compatibilist conditions. In those cases, I do not seem to make the erroneous assumption that denying the responsibility for the offender diminishes my love for my daughter. Why would I only make this mistake in reasoning in cases where the offender meets compatibilist conditions? For the same reason, the incompatibilist cannot complain that I believe my retributive attitudes are justified just because I have them. In cases where the offender does not meet compatibilist conditions, I am able to distinguish between my likely psychological response (retributive—the offender deserves to suffer) and my all-things-considered judgment (the offender does not deserve to suffer). If I were justifying beliefs simply on the basis of having them, then it would not matter whether the offender met compatibilist conditions—because I would feel deeply retributive either way. Upon reflection, then, there is a point where my fairness intuitions override my retributive feelings. But the point is where *compatibilists* and not incompatibilists claim it should be.

Do these observations vindicate compatibilism? In the end, I do not believe so. Thankfully, cases like this are the exception when we consider the wide range of actions that make people candidates for responsibility assignments. And in these other cases, my considered judgments do not vary according to whether the offender meets compatibilist conditions. What, then, is a metaskeptic to do? One alternative would be to adopt variantist criteria for moral responsibility (Knobe and Doris, forthcoming).[12] We might say that in cases involving grave harm to our family members, blameworthiness has compatibilist conditions, but in other cases, or when the victims are strangers, the offenders must meet sourcehood conditions or something of that nature. As noted in chapter 5, however, this approach seems unacceptably arbitrary. Why should it matter whether the victim is related to me rather than someone else? A more plausible variantist alternative might be to vary the criteria according to the nature of the offense rather than one's relationship to the victim. Conditions for murder would be compatibilist, both for

family members and strangers, whereas conditions for lesser offenses would be incompatibilist. But to my mind this position
still seems too arbitrary and counterintuitive. Indeed, heinous
crimes of a certain kind make the bad moral luck of the offenders especially vivid. In one frame of mind, it can be *easier* to ab-
solve them of responsibility for greater than for lesser offenses.
Attitudes towards child molesters serve as a prime illustration
of this conflict. On one hand, the nature of the crime pulls us in
the direction of setting sourcehood considerations aside and
blaming the criminal ("Screw the TNR principle!"). But the nature of the acts, when compared with offenses with more recognizable temptations, also makes it easier to see the criminals as
defective, victims of terrible constitutive luck. Most of us
(thankfully) do not have the slightest desire to perform such actions. The variantist approach does not achieve its conservative
aim because we have conflicting intuitions about the same cases
in *the same context*. Somewhat paradoxically, resolving these
conflicts seems to call for invariantist criteria—principled reasons to go one way rather than the other.

Finally, one may ask why the metaskeptic should not embrace
a subjectivist version of Smilansky's dualism—one that recognizes the reasonableness of both compatibilism and nihilism
about moral responsibility.[13] If my considered intuitions—and it
is considered intuitions that ultimately ground our judgments—
are pulled in both compatibilist and nihilist directions, it seems
reasonable to adopt a view that tries to combine the insights of
both. The problem, however, is the manner in which Smilansky
does the combining. He argues that compatibilist distinctions
should be recognized, that it is more unfair to punish the kleptomaniac than the common thief. But at the same time, he urges
us to recognize that compatibilist responsibility is "shallow,"

that in the ultimate sense, it is unfair to punish anyone, because none of us is responsible for having the character we have.

My considered intuitions seem too fractured to be accommodated in this manner. They do respect compatibilist distinctions—but only for certain kinds of cases. And in those cases, I feel that sourcehood considerations do not *in any way* let the criminal who harms my family member (and by extension the family members of others) off the hook. In this frame of mind, I do not see the criminal's responsibility as shallow at all. It seems just as deep as the libertarian or compatibilist imagines it to be. In another frame of mind, however, I agree with the nihilist that sourcehood considerations make all desert assignments inappropriate or irrational. My considered intuitions are simply inconsistent on this matter. I would like to think that they reflect two aspects of the truth about moral responsibility, but this does not seem to be the case.

In the end, then, eliminativism remains the position I endorse upon (tortured) reflection. Luck swallows everything.[14] Our characters are ultimately the result of factors beyond our control. Fairness dictates that one should not deserve blame or punishment for what amounts to a bad roll of the dice. The practical and ethical implications of adopting the objective attitude, while significant, are not disastrous (as some have claimed). Indeed, the benefits to human life may outweigh the costs. While this view does not reflect all of my values and considered intuitions, it reflects more of them than the available alternatives. Furthermore, the values it does reflect (fairness, compassion) are perhaps more virtuous than the one it does not (the retributive impulse), although I recognize the virtues that are associated with retribution as well. As is evident from the previous discussion, I am not brimming with confidence about this final verdict. I do not consider retributive feelings to be primitive or barbaric or an outdated relic of our evolutionary past. On the contrary, I believe retributive feelings have value; they express solidarity, love, loyalty, courage, and moral commitment.[15] It would not surprise me in the least if my "final" all-things-considered judgment about the conditions of moral responsibility undergoes further revision and modification.

A Conclusion (Sort of)

When embarking on this project, I envisioned a much more decisive conclusion. Although metaskepticism entails that no single position or theory about the conditions of moral responsibility is universally applicable, I nonetheless believed I would arrive at near certain judgments that would reflect *my* values and intuitions. I was wrong. But perhaps this unstable result is exactly what a metaskeptic should expect. The balance of intuitions about moral responsibility is a delicate one. Changes in our environment or life circumstances (having children, getting married, being the victim of a crime, losing someone you love, or simply getting older) can shift the balance in either direction. Maybe people's views about the conditions of moral responsibility change all the time, and it is philosophers, with long-standing commitments to particular theories, who are the exceptions. One thing is certain: I end my analysis more confident than ever that there are other considered judgments about the conditions of moral responsibility that are just as reasonable as my own.

Notes

INTRODUCTION

1. "U.S. Koreans Respond to Shootings," *Day to Day*, National Public Radio. April 18, 2007.
2. Citation from "Korean-American Groups Express Sorrow, Avoid Guilt: Korean-Americans Burdened with Guilt, Shame and Fear of Backlash," *Baltimore Sun*. April 21, 2007.
3. Brewington 2007.
4. The term "metaskepticism" comes from Nichols et al. (2003), who apply it to skepticism about skeptical theories in epistemology.

CHAPTER ONE: THE APPEAL TO INTUITION

1. Nichols, et al. (2003) 228.
2. Fischer and Ravizza (1998, 152) provide the following more careful formulation of this principle: "(1) p obtains and no one is even partly morally responsible for p; and (2) if p obtains, then q obtains, and no one is even partly morally responsible for the fact that if p obtains, then q obtains; then (3) q obtains, and no one is even partly morally responsible for q."
3. This passage about the beta principle, commonly called the "transfer of powerlessness principle," is in fact part of Van Inwagen's argument for incompatibilism with regard to free will. However, in his "direct argument" for the incompatibility of determinism and moral responsibility, he claims that "Rule B"—the transfer principle relating to moral responsibility—"perfectly parallels"

beta and in support of Rule B refers the reader to his defense of beta. (1983, 187–88).

4. Thanks to Eddy Nahmias and Derk Pereboom for encouraging me to develop this point..

5. See McKenna (2005) for an excellent discussion of Frankfurt cases and reasonable excuses.

6. Although according to Frankfurt, they would not be free since they could not change their first-order desire even if they wanted to.

7. See e.g., Wolf (1990), Fisher and Ravizza (1998), and McKenna and Russell (forthcoming).

8. I discuss the issue of original sin further in chapter 3.

9. See especially Vargas (forthcoming) and Vargas (2007).

10. One of the many bizarre consequences of the tremendous focus on the compatibility question is that answering it would do very little towards establishing a complete theory of responsibility.

11. Gomperz (1939) raises an early version of the challenge of disagreement, which has not, to my knowledge, been addressed.

12. Doris and Plakias (2008) offer the helpful analogy of health discourse, where it is plausible that certain areas admit of realist treatment (it might be a fact that cancer is a disease) but others do not (questions about mental health, for example).

13. Thanks to an anonymous reviewer for encouraging me to respond to this kind of complaint.

14. See Weinberg et al. (2010) for a discussion of the corrupting influence of philosophical reflection.

CHAPTER TWO: MORAL RESPONSIBILITY
AND THE CULTURE OF HONOR

1. See Miller (1997) for an excellent analysis of the revenge cultures of Saga Iceland.

2. Some of the material in this chapter is adapted from Sommers (2009a).

3. See Elster (1990) for a careful discussion of the rationality of revenge. My point here is simply that it is often not in the individual's short-term self-interest to retaliate after an offense, and often not in the individual's long-term self-interest either.

4. See chapter 4 for a more detailed examination of the origins of retribution.

5. The term "norms" refers broadly to social rules that regulate behavior within a group or culture. In addition, norms are *intrinsically motivating* (Kelly and Stich 2008), meaning that the motivation to comply with them does not depend solely on the perceived consequences of failing to do so. I would like to remain as neutral as possible on the kinds of cognitive architecture that might underlie norm acquisition (but see Kelly and Stich [2008], Sripada and Stich [2006], and Nichols [2004] for excellent overviews), except to say that norms must involve more than brute emotional responses to behavior, and that they may involve, or give rise to, *beliefs* about the kinds of behavior that are obligatory or impermissible. In chapter 4, I discuss the role of norms in generating beliefs and attitudes about moral responsibility in more detail.

6. Frank 1988, x (preface).

7. The label "institutionalized cultures," though not ideal, tries to draw attention to the institutions in the economy that permit anonymous cooperative endeavors, as well as to institutions that provide some degree of protection from criminal behavior. (Thanks to Alexandra Plakias for suggesting the label.)

8. See Feinberg (1968) for a classic analysis. See also the 2006 issue of *Midwest Studies,* which is devoted entirely to collective responsibility.

9. As I note in chapter 1, some have accused me of inconsistency on this point, claiming that my position does not allow me to condemn a practice like honor killings. But this is a mistake. It is true that my metaskepticism does not permit me to universally condemn norms that place little weight on the intentions of the women. But nothing about the position entails that one cannot condemn the broader practice of honor killings that call for the murder of suspected adulteresses whether they intended to commit the act or not. Again, the truth of metaskepticism does not entail the truth of a broader form of moral relativism.

10. See Nussbaum (2001) for a discussion of the ancient Greek notion of dikê, a form of justice that ignores facts about the agent's intentions in performing an act and even in some cases whether the agent committed the act at all. Williams (1993, 74) also analyzes

the Greek notion of responsibility, showing that it extends "beyond our normal purposes and what we intentionally do."

11. In Sommers (2009a), I explore the hypothesis that the concept of desert itself is de-emphasized in favor of norms that dictate the preservation of honor at all costs, even in cases where it is plainly not the victim's fault. I have since come to favor a "desert but no intention condition" for reasons discussed in this section.

12. Pereboom's (2001) first case in his four-case argument features this kind of overt manipulation as well. Pereboom is counting on his readers to find it intuitively obvious that the agent is not morally responsible for his immoral behavior.

13. According to Lacey (2001), this view is in sync with attitudes about moral responsibility in Victorian England.

14. The public or private nature of an act may influence how *wrong* the act is, but not how responsible the agent is for performing it.

15. Thanks to Joshua Knobe, John Doris, and Shaun Nichols for suggesting this possibility.

16. Blumenfeld's ultimate means of revenge does in part focus on the offender. She wants the shooter to recognize that her father is a human being and not merely an instrument for making a political statement (a notion that appears to be in line with Jean Hampton's justification of the "retributive idea" [Murphy and Hampton 1988]). When her mother mentions that she seems less interested in revenge, however, Blumenfeld replies, "I still want to stand up and say 'Don't fuck with the Blumenfelds.'" In the end, Blumenfeld appeals to an interesting (and rather rare) blend of both honor and desert-based norms in order to explain her behavior.

CHAPTER THREE: SHAME CULTURES, COLLECTIVIST SOCIETIES, ORIGINAL SIN, AND PHAROAH'S HARDENED HEART

1. Indeed, there is a great deal of overlap between shame cultures and honor cultures. Honor cultures are often referred to as "honor-shame" cultures, although not all shame cultures focus as strongly on avenging personal slights and insults.

2. See also Hamilton and Sanders (1992) for a discussion of guilt cultures and the psychological costs of wrongdoing.

3. Even with her famous claim that shame requires an audience, she adds the caveat "or the fantasy of an audience"—which can apply to many occasions on which we commonly feel guilt. We imagine our mothers, wives, or God watching us misbehave and our guilt stems from their imagined reactions to our behavior. See also Creighton (1990).

4. Indeed, it would be interesting to conduct a cross-cultural study that evaluates the subjects' identification with a Raskolnikov-like figure.

5. See Miller (1984) and Shweder and Bourne (1984) for excellent analyses.

6. Consider Susan Wolf's discussion of JoJo. According to the deep self view, JoJo meets the sufficient conditions and so is morally responsible—period. But according to Wolf, Jojo is not morally responsible—period. He does not meet her necessary condition of sanity. There is no in-between option under consideration.

7. Indeed, this intuition seems to drive Rule B in Van Inwagen's (1983) direct argument for incompatibilism.

8. See especially Edwards (1957 [1858]), 157–58.

9. See the discussion in chapters 5 and 6 of Vargas's (2005, 2007) revisionist approach to moral responsibility.

Chapter Four: Can the Variation Be Explained Away?

1. See also DePaul (2006) for a description of how to evaluate whether a judge is competent.

2. See Sommers (2009a) for another application of Mackie's argument to debates about moral responsibility. Thanks to Don Loeb for suggesting the comparison. See Loeb (1998) and Doris and Plakias (2008) for excellent discussions regarding the argument from disagreement in metaethics.

3. See Miller (1997, 1993) for full descriptions of these norms.

4. Thanks to Adam Feltz for introducing me to this phrase.

5. This is in line with the dual process theory of moral judgment developed by Greene et al. (2001, 2004).

6. Thanks to an anonymous referee for raising this objection.

7. Of course, suitably adjusted, these remarks would apply equally well to the overconfident universalist on the collectivist side of the spectrum as well.

8. See the discussion in chapter 1 concerning why the truth of metaskepticism does not entail the truth of a broader form of moral skepticism or relativism. In my view, one might plausibly argue that many practices, such as honor killings, are not justifiable no matter what society one lives in. As William Ian Miller (one of the world's biggest fans of honor cultures) notes, many features have to be in place in order for honor norms to function properly (Miller 2006). In some radical Islamic honor societies, life has been devalued "to the zero point," and principles associated with honor can only function properly when life is expensive. According to Miller, the inner cities do not produce well-functioning honor cultures either, because there are not enough "old men with property who have the power to threaten, bribe and control the young men who hold their community captive" (Miller 2006, 200), and so there is no one to keep the violence within respectable limits. When all the features of a well-ordered honor culture are in place, however, norms that de-emphasize the control condition and knowledge condition may be well calibrated to their environments—and, consequently, there would be no grounds for calling such norms irrational or immoral. If the same cannot be said for other practices, then those practices may plausibly be universally condemned as immoral.

CHAPTER FIVE: WHERE DO WE GO FROM HERE?

1. For Strawson, the necessary condition is impossible to meet (we must be *causa sui*, or self-created). For Pereboom, the necessary condition requires the agent to fulfill a control condition that is metaphysically possible but empirically implausible.

2. Thanks to an anonymous referee for raising this concern.

3. Those who do not agree with this analysis may regard Part One as an attempt to provide a novel argument for denying moral responsibility.

4. See chapter 6 of Double (1991).

5. See chapter 4 of this book for a discussion of how this strategy can apply to the moral responsibility debate.

6. See Duff (1996). Duff notes that the "retributivist revival" in the 1970's stemmed in part from the perceived moral failings of consequentialist justifications. Retributivist theories attempt to provide an "intrinsically appropriate" response to crime—but the response can only be directed at the offender.

CHAPTER SIX: A METASKEPTICAL ANALYSIS OF
LIBERTARIANISM AND COMPATIBILISM

1. In Sommers (2005), I observed that denying moral responsibility took most of the fun out of watching sports—and that in this arena, I was willing to suspend disbelief. During my dissertation defense, Galen Strawson noted that "it almost seemed as if I was serious about sports being the most difficult place to rid myself of a belief in moral responsibility." The reason it almost seemed that way was because I was serious.

2. Another option might be Smilansky's "illusionism," in which one finds libertarianism to be false but embraces the illusion that we have libertarian free will because of the moral benefits. It is unclear to me, however, to what extent this would count as an illusion—since the axiological case for "unillusioned" libertarianism relies in large part on pragmatic and moral considerations.

3. As Kane notes, this example has many parallels with Nozick's (1974) "experience machine" thought experiment.

4. Baumeister et al. (2009, 267) have expanded upon these results in a study which suggests that inducing disbelief in free will leads to an increase in aggression and a reduction in willingness to help. They also tested for "chronic disbelief" in free will and observed a correlation between high scores on this scale and a lack of helpfulness.

5. Having one's entire worldview shaken up can certainly have some short-term negative effects on behavior. Fifteen minutes after Grady Little inexplicably allowed Pedro Martinez to give up the lead to the Yankees in game 7 of the 2003 ALCS, I might have com-

mitted acts that are far more immoral than cheating on a psychology quiz.

6. I do not discuss the value of metaphysically open futures since they are, in my view, an utterly bizarre thing to want—a bit like wanting to be buried in outer space. Clearly, the weight given to the benefits and costs of each position is a subjective matter.

7. I use the vague "bound up" language to avoid taking a stand on whether the reactive attitudes constitute or presuppose the existence of moral responsibility. Either interpretation can apply in the following discussion.

8. Darwin, *Notebooks* (1836–1844) 608.

9. Thanks to an anonymous referee for throwing this monkey wrench into my argument.

10. See e.g., Nahmias et al. (2006), Nichols and Knobe (2007), and Feltz and Cokely (2009). Sommers (2010) provides a review and critique of this literature. For reasons discussed below, I do not appeal to the studies in this literature as a means of supporting one side or the other.

11. Much of the following discussion comes from Sommers (2010).

CHAPTER SEVEN: A VERY TENTATIVE
METASKEPTICAL ENDORSEMENT OF ELIMINATIVISM
ABOUT MORAL RESPONSIBILITY

1. Nagel (1979), 37.

2. "Either we are capable of being morally responsible for our behavior or we are not; metaphysical reality does not tailor itself to our hopes and needs" (Sommers, 2007a, 341).

3. Much of this section is adapted from Sommers (2007a). See also Waller (1990), Strawson (1986) and especially Pereboom (2001) for other analyses of the reactive attitudes and how they are affected by the denial of moral responsibility.

4. I call Sally a 'nihilist' here rather than an "eliminativist" to distinguish her from a metaskeptic who rejects moral responsibility. Sally (like Pereboom or Galen Strawson) is a first-order skeptic.

5. See Pereboom (2001, 201) for a similar analysis of the type

of forgiveness that is compatible with the denial of moral responsibility.

6. It is also worth noting that the objective attitude may have some benefits for married life. In and episode of *The Simpsons*, Marge tells her daughter, "Marriage is a wonderful thing. But it's also a constant battle for moral superiority." When we take the objective attitude towards our spouses, we have a much better chance of reaching a cease-fire.

7. Ross and Shestowsky (2003, 1114–15) employ the analogy of medicine for similar purposes, arguing that our policies should reflect the truths about curing illness even when the truths are counterintuitive.

8. See Kahane (2011) for an illuminating discussion of evolutionary debunking arguments in metaethics.

9. I first raised this issue in a post on the great free will blog *The Garden of Forking Paths*, entitled "[To Hell With] the TNR Principle!" February 1, 2009. The discussion that followed was enormously helpful.

10. Comments on "[To Hell With] the TNR Principle!" February 4, 2009.

11. Comments on "[To Hell With] the TNR Principle!" February 4, 2009. "You" and "your" is substituted for "Jack" and "Jack's. Jack was a stand-in in the post for my own experience.

12. See chapter 5 for a more detailed discussion of variantism and its relationship to metaskepticism.

13. See Smilansky (2000) for a detailed defense of this position.

14. This is the title of Galen Strawson's essay on free will in the *Times Literary Supplement.*

15. I do not, however, endorse rationalist justifications of retribution in the philosophy of punishment, most of which seem to be incoherent or post-hoc rationalizations of these feelings. The only viable form of retributivism, in my view, is one that is grounded in feelings and intuitions. But that is a topic for another book.

Bibliography

Audi, R. 2007. *Moral value and human diversity.* Oxford University Press.

Balicki, A. 1970. *The Netsilik Eskimo.* Natural History Press.

Baumeister, R. F., E. J. Masicampo, and C. N. DeWall. 2009. Prosocial benefits of feeling free: Disbelief in free will increases aggression and reduces helpfulness. *Personality and Social Psychology Bulletin* 35 (2):260.

Benedict, R. 2005 [1946]. *The chrysanthemum and the sword: Patterns of Japanese culture.* Mariner Books.

Bennett, J. 1980. Accountability. *Philosophical Subjects*:14–47.

Blumenfeld, L. 2002. *Revenge: A story of hope.* Washington Square Press.

Boehm, C. 1984. *Blood revenge: The anthropology of feuding in Montenegro and other tribal societies.* University Press of Kansas (Lawrence).

Bowman, J. 2006. *Honor: A history.* Encounter Books.

Boyd, R. 1988. How to be a moral realist. In G. Sayre-McCord, ed., *Essays on Moral Realism.* Cornell University Press.

Boyd, R., H. Gintis, S. Bowles, and P. J. Richerson. 2003. The evolution of altruistic punishment. *Proceedings of the National Academy of Sciences of the United States of America* 100 (6):3531. Reprinted in H. Gintis, S. Bowles, R. Boyd, and E. Fehr, eds. *Moral sentiments and material interests* (2005), MIT Press.

Brewington, K. 2007. Korean-American groups express sorrow, avoid guilt: Korean-Americans burdened with guilt, shame and fear of backlash. *Baltimore Sun*, April 21.

Brink, D. O. 1984. Moral realism and the sceptical arguments from disagreement and queerness. *Australasian Journal of Philosophy* 62 (2):111–25.

———. 1989. *Moral realism and the foundations of ethics.* Cambridge University Press.

Busquet, J. 1920. *Le droit de la vendetta et les paci corses*. A. Pedone.

Creighton, M. R. 1990. Revisiting shame and guilt cultures: A forty-year pilgrimage. *Ethos*:279–307.

Daly, M. and M. Wilson. 1988. *Homocide*. Aldine de Gruyter (Hawthorne, NY).

Daniels, N. 1979. Wide reflective equilibrium and theory acceptance in ethics. *Journal of Philosophy*:256–82.

Darwin, Charles. 1987. *Charles Darwin's Notebooks, 1836–1844*. Cornell University Press.

DePaul, M. Intuitions in Moral Inquiry. 2006. In *The Oxford handbook of ethical theory*, David Copp, ed. Oxford University Press.

Djilas, M. 1958. *Land Without Justice: An autobiography of his youth*. Methuen.

Dodds, E. R. 2004. *The Greeks and the irrational*. University of California Press.

Doris, J. M., J. Knobe, and R. L. Woolfolk. 2007. Variantism about responsibility. *Philosophical Perspectives* 21 (1):183.

Doris, J. M. and A. Plakias. 2008. How to argue about disagreement: Evaluative diversity and moral realism. In W. Sinnott-Armstrong, ed., *Moral Psychology*, vol. 2. MIT Press.

Doris, J. and S. Stich. 2005. As a matter of fact: Empirical perspectives on ethics. In *The Oxford Handbook of Contemporary Philosophy*, 114–52. Oxford University Press.

Double, R. 1991. *The non-reality of free will*: Oxford University Press (New York).

———. 1996. Honderich on the consequences of determinism. *Philosophy and Phenomenological Research* 56 (4):847–54.

———. 2002. The moral hardness of libertarianism. *Philo: A Journal of Philosophy* 5 (2). Online journal.

———. 2003. When subjectivism matters. *Metaphilosophy* 34 (4):510–23.

Duff, R. A. 1996. Penal communications: Recent work in the philosophy of punishment. *Crime & Justice* 20:1.

Edwards, Jonathan. 1958 [1754]. *Freedom of the will. His works*, vol. 1. Yale University Press.

Edwards, P. 2002. Hard and soft determinism. In *Free will*, R. Kane, ed., 59–67. Blackwell.

Ekstrom, L. W. 2000. *Free will: A philosophical study*. Westview Press.

Elster, J. 1990. Norms of revenge. *Ethics* 100:862–85.

Fehr, E. and U. Fischbacher. 2004. Third-party punishment and social norms. *Evolution and Human Behavior* 25 (2):63–87.

Fehr, E. and S. Gachter. 2002. Altruistic punishment in humans. *Nature* 415:137–40.

Feinberg, J. 1968. Collective responsibility. *Journal of Philosophy* 65:674–88.

Feltz, A. and E. T. Cokely. 2009. Do judgments about freedom and responsibility depend on who you are? Personality differences in intuitions about compatibilism and incompatibilism. *Consciousness and Cognition* 18 (1):342–50.

Fischer, J. M., R. Kane, D. Pereboom, and M. Vargas. 2007. *Four views on free will*. Wiley-Blackwell.

Fischer, John Martin, and Mark Ravizza. 1998. *Responsibility and control: A theory of moral responsibility*, Cambridge studies in philosophy and law. Cambridge University Press (Cambridge, New York).

Franco, Z., and P. G. Zimbardo, P. G. 2006–2007. The banality of heroism: Greater good. *Magazine of the Berkeley Center for the Development of Peace and Well-Being* (Fall/Winter 2006–2007): 30–35.

Frank, R. H. 1988. *Passions within reason: The strategic role of the emotions*. Norton.

Frankfurt, H. G. 1969. Alternate possibilities and moral responsibility. *Journal of Philosophy* 66:829–39.

———. 1971. Freedom of the will and the concept of a person. *Journal of Philosophy* 68:5–20.

Geertz, C. 1973. *The interpretation of cultures*. Basic Books.

Gellner, E. 1983. *Muslim society*. Cambridge University Press.

Ginat, J. 1997. *Blood revenge: Family outcasting, mediation, and honor*, 2nd edition. Sussex University Press (Brighton).

Gomperz, H. 1939. Individual, collective, and social responsibility. *Ethics* 49 (3):329–42.

Greene, J. D., and J. D. Cohen. 2004. For the law, neuroscience changes nothing and everything. *Philosophical Transactions of the Royal Society of London B*, (Special Issue on Law and the Brain) 359:1775–78.

Greene, J. D., R. B. Sommerville, L. E. Nystrom, J. M. Darley, and J. D. Cohen. 2001. An fMRI investigation of emotional engagement in moral judgment. *Science* 293 (5537):2105.

Haidt, J . 2001. The emotional dog and its rational tail: A social intuitionist approach to moral judgment. *Psychological Review* 108:814–34.

Haji, I. 1999. Moral anchors and control. *Canadian Journal of Philosophy* 29:175–203.

———. 2002. *Deontic morality and control.* Cambridge University Press.

Hamilton, V. L., and J. Sanders. 1981. The effect of roles and deeds on responsibility judgments: The normative structure of wrongdoing. *Social Psychology Quarterly* 44 (3):237–54.

———. 1992. *Everyday justice.* Yale University Press.

Hamilton, V. L., J. Sanders, Y. Hosoi, Z. Ishimura, N. Matsubara, H. Nishimura, N. Tomita, and K. Tokoro. 1988. Punishment and the individual in the United States and Japan. *Law & Society Review* 22 (2):301–28.

Harman, G. 1977. *The nature of morality.* Oxford University Press (New York).

Hasluck, M.M.H. 1954. *The unwritten law in Albania.* Cambridge University Press.

Heider, F. 1958. *The psychology of interpersonal relations.* Wiley (New York).

Henrich, J., R. Boyd, S. Bowles, C. Camerer, E. Fehr, and H. Gintis. 2004. *Foundations of human sociality: Economic experiments and ethnographic evidence from fifteen small-scale societies.* Oxford University Press.

Henrich, J., S. J. Heine, and A. Norenzayan. 2010. The weirdest people in the world. *Behavioral and Brain Sciences* 33:61–83.

Hofstede, G. 2001. *Culture's consequences: Comparing values, behaviors, institutions, and organizations across nations.* Sage Publications.

Honderich, T. 1988. *A theory of determinism.* Oxford University Press (New York).

———. 1993. *How free are you?* Oxford University Press.

———. 1996. Compatibilism, incompatibilism, and the smart aleck. *Philosophy and Phenomenological Research* 56:855–62.

Hui, C. H., and H. C. Triandis. 1986. Individualism-collectivism: A study of cross-cultural researchers. *Journal of Cross-Cultural Psychology* 17 (2):225–48.

Joyce, R. 2001. *The myth of morality.* Cambridge University Press.

———. 2006. *The evolution of morality.* MIT Press.

Kahane, G. 2011. Evolutionary debunking arguments. *Noûs* 45 (1):103–25.

Kane, R. 1996. *The significance of free will.* Oxford University Press (New York).

———. 1999. Responsibility, luck, and chance: Reflections on free will and indeterminism. *Journal of Philosophy* 96 (5):217–40.

Kant, I. 1996 [1790]. *The metaphysics of morals,* Mary Gregor, trans. Cambridge University Press (New York).

Kelly, D., and Stich, S. 2007. Two theories about the cognitive architecture underlying morality. In Peter Carruthers, Stephen Laurence, and Stephen Stich, eds., *The innate mind,* vol 3: *Foundations and future horizons,* 348–66. Oxford University Press (New York).

Kim, U., and H. S. Hakhoe. 1994. *Individualism and collectivism: Theory, method, and applications.* Sage Publications.

Knobe, J., and J. Doris. Forthcoming. Strawsonian variations: Folk morality and the search for a unified theory. *The handbook of moral psychology.* Oxford University Press.

Kundera, M. 1999. *The unbearable lightness of being.* M. H. Heim, trans. Harper Perennial Modern Classics.

Lacey, N. 2001. In search of the responsible subject: History, philosophy and social sciences in criminal law theory. *Modern Law Review* 64 (3):350–71.

Lesky, A. 1966. Decision and responsibility in the tragedy of Aeschylus. *Journal of Hellenic Studies* 86:78–85.

Lloyd-Jones, H. 1962. The guilt of Agamemnon. *Classical Quarterly* 12 (2):187–99.

Loeb, D. 1998. Moral realism and the argument from disagreement. *Philosophical Studies* 90 (3):281–303.

Lombardo, S. trans. 1997. *Iliad.* Hackett.

Luther, Martin. 2008 [1525]. *Bondage of the will.* Hendrickson Publishers (Peabody, MA).

Mackie, J. L. 1977. *Ethics: Inventing right and wrong.* Harmondsworth (London).

Mallon, R., E., Machery, S. Nichols, and S. Stich. 2009. Against arguments from reference. *Philosophy and Phenomenological Research* 79 (2):332–56.

Markus, H. R., and S. Kitayama. 1991. Culture and the self: Implications for cognition, emotion, and motivation. *Psychological Review* 98 (2): 224–53.

McCallister, W. S. 2005. The Iraq insurgency: Anatomy of a tribal rebellion. *First Monday* 10:3–10.

McGrath, S. 2008. Moral disagreement and moral expertise. *Oxford Studies in Metaethics* 3:87–108.

McKenna, M. 2005. Where Strawson and Frankfurt Meet. *Midwest Studies in Philosophy* 29:163–80.

McKenna, M. and P. Russell. Forthcoming. *Free will and reactive attitudes.* Ashgate.

Mele, A. 1995. *Autonomous agents.* Oxford University Press.

———. 1999. Kane, luck, and the significance of free will. *Philosophical Explorations* 2 (2):96–104.

———. 2005. A critique of Pereboom's "four-case argument" for incompatibilism. *Analysis* 65 (285):75–80.

Merida, K. 2006. In or out of the game? *Washington Post,* December 31.

Miller, J. G. 1984. Culture and the development of everyday social explanation. *Journal of Personality and Social Psychology* 46 (5):961–78.

Miller, W. I. 1993. *Humiliation: And other essays on honor, social discomfort, and violence.* Cornell University Press.

———. 1997. *Bloodtaking and peacemaking: Feud, law, and society in saga Iceland.* University of Chicago Press.

———. 2006. *Eye for an eye.* Cambridge University Press.

Murphy, J., and J. Hampton. 1988. *Forgiveness and mercy.* Cambridge University Press.

Nadelhoffer, T., and A. Feltz. 2007. Folk intuitions, slippery slopes, and necessary fictions: An Essay on Saul Smilansky's free will illusionism. *Midwest Studies in Philosophy* 31 (1):202.

Nagel, Thomas. 1979. *Mortal questions.* Cambridge University Press.

Nahmias, E., D. J. Coates, and T. Kvaran. 2007. Free will, moral responsibility, and mechanism: Experiments on folk intuitions. *Midwest Studies in Philosophy* 31 (1):214–42.

Nahmias, E., S. G. Morris, T. Nadelhoffer, and J. Turner. 2006. Is incompatibilism intuitive? *Philosophy and Phenomenological Research* 73 (1):28–53.

Nahmias, E., and D. Murray. 2010. Experimental philosophy on free will: An error theory for incompatibilist intuitions. In *New waves in the philosophy of action,* Jesús Aguilar, Andrei buckareff, and Keith Frankish, eds., 189–216. Palgrave Macmillan.

Nichols, Shaun. 2004. *Sentimental rules: On the natural foundations of moral judgment.* Oxford University Press.

——. 2007. After incompatibilism: A naturalistic defense of the reactive attitudes. *Philosophical Perspectives* 21 (1):405.

Nichols, S., and J. Knobe. 2007. Moral responsibility and determinism: The cognitive science of folk intuitions. *Noûs* 41 (4):663.

Nichols, S., S. Stich, and J. Weinberg,. 2003. Metaskepticism: Meditations in ethno-epistemology. In *The skeptics,* S. Luper, ed., 227–47. Ashgate (Burlington, VT).

Nietzsche, F. W. 1992 [1887]. *On the genealogy of morals.* W. A. Kaufmann, trans. Vintage.

Nisbett, R. E., and D. Cohen. 1996. *Culture of honor: The psychology of violence in the South.* Westview Press.

Nozick, R. 1974. *Anarchy, state, and utopia.* Basic Books.

Nussbaum, M. 1985. Aeschylus and practical conflict. *Ethics* 95 (2):233–67.

——. 1993. Equity and mercy. *Philosophy and Public Affairs* 22 (2):83–125.

——. 2001. *The fragility of goodness: Luck and ethics in Greek tragedy and philosophy.* Cambridge University Press.

O'Connor, T. 2000. Causality, mind, and free will. *Noûs* 34 (s14):105–17.

Pereboom, D. 1995. Determinism al dente. *Noûs* 29 (1):21–45.

——. 2001. *Living without free will:* Cambridge University Press.

——. 2008. A compatibilist account of the epistemic conditions on rational deliberation. *The Journal of Ethics* 12 (3):287–306.

Rawls, John. 1972. *A theory of justice.* Clarendon Press.

Rea, M. C. 2007. The metaphysics of original sin. In *Persons: Human and divine,* D. Zimmerman and P. van Inwagen, eds., 319–56. Oxford University Press.

Richerson, P., and R. Boyd. 2005. *Not by genes alone.* University of Chicago Press.

Ross, L., and D. Shestowsky. 2003. Contemporary psychology's challenges to legal theory and practice. *Northwestern University Law Review* 97:1081.Ruse, M. 1986. *Taking Darwin seriously.* Blackwell.

Russell, B. 2004. *History of western philosophy.* Routledge.

Russell, P. 1992. Strawson's way of naturalizing responsibility. *Ethics* 102 (2):287–302.

———. 1995. *Freedom and moral sentiment*. Oxford University Press.

Salzman, P. C. 2008. *Culture and conflict in the Middle East*. Humanity Books.

Sharma, R. K., and R. M. Sharma. 1997. *Anthropology*. Atlantic Books.

Shweder, R. A., and E. J. Bourne. 1984. Does the concept of the person vary cross-culturally? In *Culture theory: Essays on mind, self, and emotion*, R. A. Shweder and R. A. LeVine, eds., 158–99. Cambridge University Press.

Shweder, R. A., and J. G. Miller. 1985. The social construction of the person: How is it possible. In *The social construction of the person*, K. J. Gergen and K. Davis, eds., 41–69. Springer (New York).

Singer, T., et al. 2006. Empathic neural responses are modulated by the perceived fairness of others. *Nature* 439:466–69.

Smilansky, S. 2000. *Free will and illusion*. Oxford University Press (New York).

———. 2010. Free will: Some bad news. In *Action, ethics, and responsibility*, J. K. Campbell, M. O'Rourke, and H. S. Silverstein, eds., 187–202. MIT Press.

Smith, M. A. 1994. *The moral problem*. Wiley-Blackwell.

Sommers, T. 2005. *Beyond freedom and resentment: An error theory of free will and moral responsibility*. PhD diss., Duke University.

———.2007a . The objective attitude. *Philosophical Quarterly* 57 (228): 321–41.

———. 2007b. The illusion of freedom evolves. *Distributed cognition and the will*. In *Distributed cognition and the will*, David Spurrett, Harold Kincaid, Don Ross, and Lynn Stephens, eds. MIT Press.

———. 2009a. The two faces of revenge: moral responsibility and the culture of honor. *Biology & Philosophy* 24 (1):35–50.

———. 2009b. More work for hard incompatibilism. *Philosophy and Phenomenological Research* 79 (3):511–21.

———.2010. Experimental philosophy and free will." *Philosophy Compass* 5:199–-212. Online journal.

Speak, D. 2004. Toward an axiological defense of libertarianism. *Philosophical Topics* 32 (1/2):353.

Spence, J. T. 1985. Achievement American style: The rewards and costs of individualism. *American Psychologist* 40 (12):1285–95.

Sripada, C. S., and S. Stich. 2006. A framework for the psychology of norms. In Peter Carruthers, Stephen Laurence, and Stephen Stich, eds., *The innate mind: Culture and cognition.* 280–301. Oxford University Press (New York).

Strawson, G. 1986. *Freedom and belief.* Clarendon Press.

———. 1994. The impossibility of moral responsibility. *Philosophical Studies* 75 (1):5–24.

Strawson, P. F. 2003 [1962]. Freedom and resentment. In G. Watson, ed., *Free will,* 72–93. Oxford University Press.

Sturgeon, N., and D. Copp. 2005. Ethical naturalism. In *Oxford Handbook of Ethical Theory* 1 (9):91–122.

Triandis, H. C. 1989. Cross-cultural studies of individualism and collectivism. *Nebraska Symposium on Motivation,* 37:41–133.

———. 1995. *Individualism and collectivism.* Westview Press.

Triandis, H. C., R. Bontempo, M. J., Villareal, M. Asai, and N. Lucca. 1988. Individualism and collectivism—Cross-cultural perspectives on the self in group relationships. *Journal of Personality and Social Psychology* 54 (2):323–38.

Trivers, R. L. 1971. The evolution of reciprocal altruism. *Quarterly Review of Biology* 46 (1):35.

Van Inwagen, P. 1983. *An essay on free will.* Oxford University Press (New York).

———. 2000. Free will remains a mystery. *Philosophical Perspectives* 14:1-20.

Vargas, M. 2004. Responsibility and the aims of theory: Strawson and revisionism. *Pacific Philosophical Quarterly* 85 (2):218–41.

———. 2005. The revisionist's guide to responsibility. *Philosophical Studies* 125 (3):399–429.

———. 2007. Revisionism. In J. Fischer, R. Kane, D. Pereboom, and M. Vargas, *Four views on free will,* 126–65. Blackwell.

———. 2009. Revisionism about free will: A statement and defense. *Philosophical Studies* 144 (1):45–62.

———. Forthcoming. *Building better beings: A theory of moral responsibility.* Oxford University Press.

Vohs, K. D., and J. W. Schooler. 2008. The value of believing in free will. *Psychological Science* 19:49–54.

Wallace, R. J. 1994. *Responsibility and the moral sentiments.* Harvard University Press.

Waller, B. N. 1990. *Freedom without responsibility.* Temple University Press.

———. 1998. *The natural selection of autonomy.* SUNY Press.

Watson, G. 1975. Free agency. *Journal of Philosophy* 72:205–220.

Weinberg, J. et al. 2010. Are philosophers expert intuiters? *Philosophical Psychology* 23 (3):331–55.

Wiggins, D. 1973. Towards a reasonable libertarianism. In T. Honderich, ed., *Essays on freedom of action,* 33–61. Routledge and Kegan Paul.

Williams, B. 1993. Shame and necessity. University of California Press.

Wolf, S. 1981. The importance of free will. *Mind* 90:386–405.

———. 1987. Sanity and the metaphysics of responsibility. In *Responsibility, character, and the emotions,* F. Schoeman, ed., 46–62. Cambridge University Press.

———. 1990. *Freedom within reason:* Oxford University Press (New York).

Woolfolk, R. L., J. M. Doris, and J. M. Darley. 2006. Identification, situational constraint, and social cognition: Studies in the attribution of moral responsibility. *Cognition* 100 (2):283–301.

Zakaria, F., and Lee Kuan Yew. 1994. Culture is destiny: A conversation with Lee Kuan Yew. *Foreign Affairs* 73 (2):109–26. Available online at: http://www.foreignaffairs.com/articles/49691/fareed-zakaria/a-conversation-with-lee-kaun-yew.

Index